James Parton

Smoking and Drinking

James Parton

Smoking and Drinking

ISBN/EAN: 9783743313866

Manufactured in Europe, USA, Canada, Australia, Japa

Cover: Foto ©ninafisch / pixelio.de

Manufactured and distributed by brebook publishing software (www.brebook.com)

James Parton

Smoking and Drinking

PREFACE.

THE next very important thing that man has to attend to is his health.

In some other respects, progress has been made during the last hundred years, and several considerable obstacles to the acquisition of a stable happiness have been removed or diminished.

In the best parts of the best countries, so much knowledge is now freely offered to all the young as suffices to place within their reach all existing knowledge. We may say with confidence that the time is not distant when, in the United States, no child will live farther than four miles from a school-house, kept open four months in the year, and when there will be the beginning of a self-sustaining public library in every town and village of a thousand inhabitants. This great business of making knowledge universally accessible is well in hand ; it has gone so far that it must go on till the work is complete.

In this country, too, if nowhere else, there is so near an approach to perfect freedom of thinking, that scarcely any one, whose conduct is good, suffers inconvenience from professing any extreme or eccentricity of mere opinion. I constantly meet, in New England villages, men who differ as widely as possible from their neighbors on the most dividing of all subjects ; but if they are good citizens and good neighbors, I have never observed that they were the less esteemed on that account. Their peculiarities of opinion become as familiar as the color of their hair, or the shape of their every-day hat, and as inoffensive. This is a grand triumph of good sense and good nature; or, as Matthew Arnold would say, of the metropolitan over the provincial spirit. It is also recent. It was not the case fifty years ago. It was not the case twenty years ago.

The steam-engine, and the wondrous machinery which the steam-engine moves, have so cheapened manufactured articles, that a mechanic, in a village, may have so sufficient a share of the comforts, conveniences, and decencies of life, that it is sometimes hard to say what real advantage his rich neighbor has over him. The rich man used to have one truly enviable advantage over others: his family was safer, in case of his sudden death. But a mechanic, who has his home paid for, his life insured, and a year's subsistence accumulated, is as secure in this respect as, perhaps, the nature of human affairs admits. Now, an American workingman, anywhere out of a few largest cities, can easily have all these safeguards around his family by the time he is forty; and few persons can be rich before they are forty.

We may say, perhaps, speaking generally, that, in the United States, there are no formidable obstacles to the attainment of substantial welfare, except such as exist in the nature of things and in ourselves.

But in the midst of so many triumphs of man over material and immaterial things, man himself seems to dwindle and grow pale. Not here only, but in all the countries that have lately become rich enough to buy great quantities of the popular means of self-destruction, and in which women cease to labor as soon as their husbands and parents acquire a little property, and in which children sit in school and out of school from five to nine hours a **day,** and in which immense numbers of people breathe impure air twenty-two hours out of every twenty-four. In the regions of the United States otherwise most highly favored, nearly every woman, under forty, is sick or sickly; and hardly any young man has attained a proper growth, and measures the proper size around the chest. As to the young girls and school-children, if, in a school or party of two hundred, you can pick out thirty well-developed, well-proportioned, robust, ruddy children, you will do better than I have sometimes been able to do.

This begins to alarm and puzzle all but the least reflective persons. People begin to wonder why every creature, whether of native or foreign origin, should flourish in America, except man.

Not that there is anything mysterious with regard to the immediate causes of this obvious decline in the health and robustness of the race. Miss Nightingale tells **us** that more than half of all the sickness in the world comes of breathing bad air. She speaks feelingly of the time, not long passed, when the winds of heaven played freely through every house, from Windsor Castle to the laborer's cottage, and when every lady put forth muscular effort in the polishing of surfaces. That was the time when bread was an article of diet, and the Devil had not invented hot biscuit. The agreeable means of self-destruction, now so cheap and universal, were unknown, or very costly; and the great mass of the people subsisted, necessarily, upon the plain fare which affords abundant nourishment, without overtasking the digestive powers. Terrible epidemics, against which the medical science of the **time vainly** contended, swept off weakly persons, shortened the average duration of life, and raised the standard of health.

But now we can **all pervert and poison** ourselves if we

will, and yet not incur much danger of prompt extinction. Indeed, it is hard for the most careful and resolute person to avoid being a party to the universal violation of natural law. Children, of course, are quite helpless. How could I help, at eight years of age, being confined six hours a day in a school, where the word "ventilation" was only known as an object of spelling? How could I help, on Sunday, being entombed in a Sunday-school room, eight or nine feet high, crowded with children, all breathing their utmost? I hated it. I loathed it. I protested against it. I played truant from it. But I was thirteen years old before I could escape that detested basement, where I was poisoned with pernicious air, and where well-intentioned Ignorance made **virtue** disgusting, contemptible, and ridiculous, by turns.

As all our virtues support one another, so all the vices of modern **life are** allies. Smoking **and** drinking are effects, as well as causes. We waste **our** vital force; we make larger demands upon ourselves **than** the nature of the human constitution warrants, and then we crave the momentary, delusive, pernicious aid which tobacco and alcohol afford. I suppose the use of these things will increase or decrease, as man degenerates or improves.

This subject, I repeat, is the next great matter upon which we have to throw ourselves. The republication of these essays is only to be justified **on** the ground that every little helps.

I think, **too, that** the next new sensation enjoyed by the self-indulgent, self-destroying inhabitants of the wealthy nations will **be** the practice of virtue. I mean, **of** course, the real thing, now nearly forgotten, the beginning of which is self-control, and which leads people to be temperate **and** pure, and enables them to go contrary to custom **and** fashion, without being eccentric **or** violent about it.

That kind of virtue, I mean, which enables us to accept hard duties, and perform them with cheerful steadfastness; which enables us to make the most of our own lives, and to rear glorious offspring, superior to ourselves.

It is surprising what a new interest is given to life by denying ourselves one vicious indulgence. What luxury so luxurious as just self-denial! Who has ever seen any happy people that were not voluntarily carrying a heavy burden? Human nature is so formed to endure and to deny itself, that those mistaken souls who forsake the world, and create for themselves artificial woes, and impose upon themselves unnecessary tasks, and deny themselves rational and beneficial pleasures, are a thousand times happier than those self-indulgent and aimless men, whom we see every afternoon, gazing listlessly out of club-windows, wondering why it is so long to six o'clock.

I heard a young man say, the other day, that smoking had been the bane of his life, but that after abstaining for seven months, during which he made no progress in overcoming the desire to smoke, he had come to the conclusion that he was past cure, and must needs go on, as long as he lived. He *was* going on, when he made the remark, smoking a pipe half as big and twice as yellow as himself. It was a great pity. That daily longing to smoke, with the daily triumphant struggle against it, was enough of itself to make his life both respectable and interesting. During those seven months, he was a man. He could claim fellowship with all the noble millions of our race, who have waged a secret warfare with Desire, all the days of their lives. If he had kept on, if he had not lapsed under the domination of his tyrant, he would probably have ascertained what there was in his way of life which kept alive in him the craving for stimulation. In all probability, he would have conquered the desire at last.

And such a victory is usually followed by others similar. The cigar and the bottle are often replaced by something not sensual. The brain, freed from the dulling, lowering influence, regains a portion of its natural vivacity; and that vivacity frequently finds worthy objects upon which to expend itself.

NEW YORK, September, 1868.

SMOKING.

BY AN OLD SMOKER.

I HAVE sometimes thought that there are people whom it does pay to smoke: those hod-carriers on the other side of the street, for example. It cannot be a very pleasant thing to be a hod-carrier at this season of the year, when a man who means to be at work at seven A. M. must wake an hour before the first streak of dawn. There is an aged sire over there, who lives in Vandewater Street, which is two miles and a quarter from the building he is now assisting to erect. He must be astir by half past five, in order to begin his breakfast at six; and at half past six he is in the car, with his dinner-kettle in his hand, on his way up town. About the time when the more active and industrious readers of this magazine begin to think it is nearly time to get up, this father of a family makes his first ascent of the ladder with a load of mortar on his shoulder. At twelve, the first stroke of the bell of St. George's Church (it is New York where these interesting events occur) sets him at liberty, and he goes in quest of his kettle. On proprietor's overcoat to keep the cold dinner from freezing stiff. But we will imagine a milder day, when the group of hod-carriers take their kettles to some sunny, sheltered spot about the building, where they sit upon soft, commodious boards, and enjoy their repast of cold meat and bread. The homely meal being concluded, our venerable friend takes out his short black pipe for his noontide smoke. How he enjoys it! How it seems to rest him! It is a kind of conscious sleep, ending, perhaps, in a brief unconscious sleep, from which he wakes refreshed for another five hours of the heavy hod.

Who could wish to deny a poor man a luxury so cheap, and so dear? It does not cost him more than ten cents a week; but so long as he has his pipe, he has a sort of refuge to which he can fly from trouble. Especially consoling to him is it in the evening, when he is in his own crowded and most uninviting room. The smoke that is supposed to "poison the air" of some apartments seems to correct the foulness of this; and the smoker appears to be a benefactor to all its inmates, as well as to those who pass its door.

Besides, this single luxury of smoke, at a cost of one cent and three sevenths per diem, is the full equivalent of all the luxuries which wealth can buy! None but a smoker, or one who has been a smoker, can realize this truth; but it is a truth. That short black pipe does actually place the hod-carrier, so far as mere luxury goes, on a par with Commodore Vanderbilt or the Prince of Wales. Tokay, champagne, turtle, game, and all the other luxurious commodities are not, taken altogether, so much to those who can daily enjoy them, as poor Paddy's pipe is to him. Indeed, the few rich people with whose habits I chance to be acquainted seldom touch such things, and never touch them except to please others. They all appear to go upon the system of the late Lord Palmerston, who used to say to his new butler, "Provide for my guests whatever the season affords; but for *me* there must be always a leg of mutton and an apple-pie." Let the Prince of Wales (or any other smoker) be taken to a banqueting-hall, the tables **of** which should be spread with all the dainties which persons of wealth are erroneously supposed to be continually consuming, but over the door let there be written the terrible words, "No smoking." Then show him an adjoining room, with a table **exhibiting** Lord Palmerston's leg of mutton and apple-pie, plus a bundle of cigars. If any one doubts which **of** these two feasts the Prince of Wales would choose, we tell that doubting individual he has never been a smoker.

Now the short pipe of the hod-carrier is just as good to him as the regalias could be that cost two hundred dollars a thousand in Havana, and sixty cents each in New York. If you were to give him one of those regalias, he would prefer to cut it up and smoke it in his pipe, and then he would **not** find it as good as the tobacco he usually smokes. The poor laborer's pipe, therefore, is a potent equalizer. To the enjoyment of pleasures purely luxurious there is a limit which is soon reached; and I maintain that a poor man gets as much of this *kind* of pleasure out of his pipe as a prince or a railroad king can extract from all the costly wines and viands of the table.

If there is a man in the world who ought to smoke, that ancient hod-carrier is the man. A stronger case for smoking cannot be selected from ordinary life. Does it pay him? After an attentive and sympathetic consideration of his case, I am compelled reluctantly to conclude that it does not.

The very fact that it tends to make him contented with his lot is a point against his pipe. It is a shame to him to be contented. To a young man the carrying of the hod is no dishonor, for it is fit that young men should bear burdens and perform lowly tasks. But the hod is not for gray hairs. Whenever, in this free and spacious America, we see a man past fifty carrying heavy loads upon his shoulders, or performing any hired labor that requires little skill or thought, we know that there must have been some great defect or waste in that man's life. The first dollar that George Law ever earned, after leaving his father's house, was earned by carrying the hod at Albany. But with that dollar he bought an arithmetic and spelling-book; which, when winter closed in and put a stop to hod-carrying, he mastered, and thus began to prepare to build the "High Bridge" over the Harlem River, where he made a million dollars by using steam hod-carriers instead of Irish ones. The pipe is one of the points of difference between the hod-carrier content with his lot and the hod-carrier who means to get into bricklaying next spring. Yonder is one of the latter class reading his " Sun " after dinner, instead of steeping his senses in forgetfulness over a pipe. He, perhaps, will be taking a contract to build a bridge over the East River, about the time when his elderly comrade is buried in a corporation coffin.

Of course, there are vigorous and triumphant men who smoke, and there are dull, contented men who do not. It is only of the general tendency of the poor man's pipe that I wish to speak. I mean to say that it tends to make him satisfied with a lot which it is his chief and immediate duty to alleviate. He ought to hate and loathe his tenement-house home; and when he goes to that home in the evening, instead of sitting down in stolid selfishness to smoke, he should be active in giving his wife (who usually has the worst of it) the assistance she needs and deserves. Better the merry song, the cheerful talk, the pleasant stroll, than this dulling of the senses and the brain in smoke. Nobler the conscious misery of such a home, than the artificial lethargy of the pipe. It is an unhandsome thing in this husband to steal out of his vile surroundings into cloudland, and leave his **wife and** children alone to their noisome desolation.

If it does not pay this hod-carrier to smoke, it pays no man. If this man cannot smoke without injustice to others, no man can.

Ladies, the **natural** enemies of tobacco, relented so far during the war as to send tobacco and pipes to the soldiers, and worked with their own fair hands many a pouch. Indeed, the pouch industry continues, though we will do the ladies the justice to say that, as their pouches usually have every excellent quality except fitness for the purpose intended, few of them ever hold tobacco. Does the lady who presented General Sheridan the other evening, in New York, with those superb and highly decorated tobacco-pouches suppose the gallant General has had, or will ever have, the heart to profane such beautiful objects with the noxious weed? It is evident from these gracious concessions on the part of the ladies, that they suppose the soldier is a man whose circumstances call imperatively for the solace of smoke; and really, when the wearied men after a long day's march gathered round the camp-fire for the evening pipe, the most infuriate hater of the weed must have sometimes paused and questioned the science which forbids the indulgence. But, reader, did you ever travel in one of the forward cars of a train returning from the seat of war, when the soldiers were coming home to re-enlist? We need not attempt to describe the indescribable scene. Most readers can imagine it. We allude to it merely as a set-off to the pleasant and picturesque spectacle of the tired soldiers smoking round the camp-fire.

In truth, the soldier is the last man in the world who should smoke; for the simple reason, that while he, more than **any other** man, has need of all his strength, smoking robs him of part of it. It is not science alone which establishes this truth. The winning boat of

Harvard University, and the losing boat of Yale, were not rowed by smokers. One of the first things demanded of a young man who is going into training for a boat-race is, *Stop smoking!* And he himself, long before his body has reached its highest point of purity and development, will become conscious of the lowering and disturbing effect of smoking one inch of a mild cigar. No smoker who has ever trained severely for a race, or a game, or a fight, needs to be told that smoking reduces the tone of the system and diminishes all the forces of the body. He *knows* it. He has been as conscious of it as a boy is conscious of the effects of his first cigar. Let the Harvard crew smoke during the last two months of their training, and **let** the Yale men abstain, and there is one individual prepared to risk a small sum upon Yale's winning back her laurels.

A soldier should be in training always. Compelled to spend nine tenths of his time in laboriously doing nothing, he is called upon occasionally, for a few hours or days or weeks, to put forth exertions which task human endurance to the uttermost. The soldier, too, of all men, should have quiet nerves; for the phantoms of war scare more men than **its** real dangers, and men's bodies can shake when their souls are firm. That two and two make four is not a truth more unquestionably certain than that smoking does diminish a soldier's power of endurance, and does make him more susceptible to imaginary dangers. **If** a regiment were to be raised for the hardest service of which men can ever be capable, and that service were to be performed for a series of campaigns, it would be necessary to exclude from the commissariat, not tobacco only, but coffee and tea. Each man, in short, would have to be kept in what prize-fighters call "condition"; by which term they simply mean the natural state of the body, uncontaminated by poison, and unimpaired by indolence or excess. Every man is in duty bound to be "in condition" at all times; but the soldier, — it is part of his profession to be "in condition." When remote posterity comes to read of the millions and millions of dollars expended during the late war in curing soldiers untouched by bayonet or bullet, the enthusiasm of readers will not be excited by the generosity displayed in bestowing those millions. People will lay down the book and exclaim: "How ignorant were our poor ancestors of the laws of life! A soldier in hospital without a wound! How extremely absurd!"

To this weighty and decisive objection minor ones may be added. The bother and vexation arising from the pipe were very great during the campaigns of the late war. Half the time the smokers, being deprived of their accustomed stimulant, were in that state of uneasy longing which smokers and other stimulators know. Men were shot during the war merely because they *would* strike a light and smoke. The desire sometimes overcame all considerations of prudence and soldierly duty. A man out on picket, of a chilly night, knowing perfectly well that lighting his pipe would have the twofold effect of revealing his presence and inviting a bullet, was often unable to resist the temptation. Many men, too, risked capture in seeking what smokers call "a little fire." A fine, stalwart officer of a Minnesota regiment, whose natural forces, if he had given nature a fair chance, would have been abundantly sufficient for him without the aid of any stimulant, has told me there were nights when he would have gladly given a month's pay for a light. Readers probably remember the incident related in the newspapers of one of our smoking generals, who, after being defeated by the enemy, heard of the arrival of gunboats which assured his safety, and promised to restore his fortunes. The *first* thing he did was to send an aid on board a gunboat to ask if they had any cigars. He was right in so doing. It was a piece of strategy necessitated by the circumstances. Let any man who has been in the habit of smoking ten to twenty cigars a day be suddenly deprived of them at a time when there is a great strain upon body and mind, and he will find himself reduced to a state bordering upon imbecility. Knowing what I know of the smoking habits of some officers of high rank, I should tremble for the success of any difficult operation, to be conducted by them in presence of an enemy, if their cigars had given out the evening before ; nor could a spy do his employers a better service than to creep into the tents of some generals the night before an engagement, and throw all their cigars and tobacco into a pail of water.

Of all men, therefore, the soldier is the very last man who could find his account in a practice which lowers the tone of his health, reduces his power of endurance, litters his knapsack, pesters him with a system of flints and tinder, and endangers his efficiency in critical moments. If all the world smoked, still the soldier should abstain.

Sailors and other prisoners experience so many dull hours, and possess so many unused faculties, that some cordial haters of tobacco have thought that such persons might be justified in a habit which only lessens what they have in superfluity. In other words, sailors, being in a situation extremely unfavorable to spiritual life, ought not merely to yield to the lowering influence of the forecastle, but add to it one more benumbing circumstance. On the contrary, they ought to strive mightily against the paralyzing effects of monotony, — not give up to them, still less aggravate them. There is no reason, in the nature of things, why a sailor, after a three years' voyage, should not step on shore a man more alert in body and mind than when he sailed, and all alive to communicate the new knowledge he has acquired and the wonders he has seen. Why should he go round this beautiful world drugged?

We must, therefore, add the sailor to the hod-carrier and the soldier, and respectfully take away his pipe. I select these classes, because they are supposed most to need artificial solace, and to be most capable of enduring the wear and tear of a vicious habit. Each of these classes also can smoke without much offending others, and each is provided with an "expectoratoon" which disgusts no one. The hod-carrier and the soldier have the earth and the sailor the ocean. But, for all that, the pipe is an injury to them. Every man of them would be better without it.

But if we must deny *them* the false solace of their pipe, what can be said of the all-but-universal smoking of persons supposed to be more refined than they, and whose occupations furnish them no pretence of an excuse? We now see painters in their studios smoking while they paint, and sculptors pegging away at the marble with a pipe in their mouths. Clergymen hurry out of church to find momentary relief for their tired throats in an ecstatic smoke, and carry into the apartment of fair invalids the odor of ex-cigars. **How** it may be in other cities I know not, but in **New** York a parishioner who wishes to confer upon his clergyman a *real* pleasure **can** hardly do a safer thing than send him a thousand cigars of a good clerical brand. It is particularly agreeable to a clergyman to receive a present which supplies him with a luxury he loves, but in which he knows in his inmost soul he ought not to indulge. **No matter** for all his **fine** arguments, there is not one clergyman in ten **that succeeds** in this short life in reducing his conscience to such a degree **of** obtuseness that **he can buy a box of** cigars (at present prices) without a qualm of self-reproach. Editors, writers for the **press**, reporters, and others who haunt the places where newspapers are made, are smokers, except a few controlling men, and a few more who are on the way to become such. Most of the authors whose names are familiar to the public smoke steadily; even the poets most beloved do so. Philosophers have taken to the pipe of late years. Mr. Dickens, they say, toys with a cigar occasionally, but can hardly be reckoned among the smokers, and never touches a cigar when he has a serious task on hand. Mr. Prescott smoked, and O, how he loved his cigar! It was he who, when his physician had limited him to one cigar a day, ran all over Paris in quest of the largest cigars that Europe could furnish. In my smoking days I should have done the same. Thackeray smoked; he was very particular in his smoking; the scent of a bad cigar was an abomination to him. That Byron smoked, and loved "the naked beauties" of tobacco, he has told us in the most alluring verses the weed has ever inspired. Milton, Locke, Raleigh, Ben Jonson, Izaak Walton, Addison, Steele, Bolingbroke, Burns, Campbell, Scott, Talfourd, Christopher North, Lamb, were all smokers at some part of their lives. Among our Presidents, John Adams, John Quincy Adams, General Jackson, and probably many others, were smokers. Daniel Webster once smoked. Henry Clay, down to a late period of his life, chewed, smoked, and took snuff, but never approved of either practice, and stopped two of them. General Grant smokes, but regrets that he does, and has reduced his daily allowance of cigars. Edwin Booth smokes, as do most of the gentlemen of his arduous profession. Probably a majority of the physicians and surgeons in the United States, under forty years of age, are smokers; and who ever knew a medical student that did not smoke furiously? This, perhaps, is not to be wondered at, since doctors live upon the bodily sins of mankind.

The question is, Does it pay these gentlemen to smoke? *They* know it does not. It would be gross arrogance in any individual to lift up his voice in rebuke of so many illustrious persons, but for the fact that there is scarcely one of them who does not feel that the practice is wrong, or, at least, absurd. Almost all confirmed smokers will go so far as to admit that they wish they had never acquired the habit. Few of them desire their boys to acquire it. None recommend it to other men. Almost all smokers, who are not Turks, Chinamen, or Indians, appreciate at once the wisdom of Sir Isaac Newton's reply to one who asked him why he never smoked a pipe. "Because," said he "I am unwilling to make to myself any necessities." Nor can any intelligent smoker doubt that the fumes of tobacco are hostile to the vital principle. We smokers and ex-smokers all remember how our first cigar sickened us; we have all experienced various ill effects from what smokers call "smoking too much"; and very many smokers have, once or twice in their lives, risen in revolt against their tyrant, given away their pipes, and lived free men long enough to become conscious that their whole being had been torpid, and was alive again. No, no! let who will deny that smoking is unfriendly to life, and friendly to all that wars upon life, smokers will not question it, unless they are very ignorant indeed, or very young. It will be of no avail to talk to *them* of the man who lived to be a hundred years old and had smoked to excess for half a century. Smokers have that within which keeps them well in mind that smoking is pernicious. If there are any smokers who doubt it, it is the few whom smoke is rapidly killing; such, for example, as the interesting professional men who smoke an excellent quality of cigars and "break down" before they are thirty-five. It is not honest, legitimate hard work that breaks so many people down in the prime of life. It is bad habits.

Smoking is a barbarism. This is the main argument against what is termed moderate smoking. There is something in the practice that allies a man with barbarians, and constantly tends to make him think and talk like a barbarian. Being at New Haven last September, a day or two before the opening of the term at Yale College, I sat in one of the public rooms of the hotel late one evening, hoping some students would come in, that I might see what sort of people college students are in these times. Yale College hath a pleasant seat. Who can stroll about upon that beautiful College Green, under those majestic elms, without envying the youth who are able to spend four long years of this troublesome life in the tranquil acquisition of knowledge amid scenes so refined and engaging?

The visitor is bewitched with a wild desire to give the college two or three million dollars immediately, to enable it to become, in all respects, what it desires, aims, and intends to become. Visions of the noble Athenian youth thronging about the sages of eld, and learning wisdom from their lips, flit through his mind, as he wanders among the buildings of the college, and dodges the colored men who are beating carpets and carrying furniture. In this exalted frame of mind, suppose the stranger seated in the room of the hotel just mentioned. In the middle of the small apartment sat one fat, good-humored, uneducated man of fifty, smoking a cigar,—about such a man as we expect to find in the "office" of a large livery stable. At half past ten a young man strolled in, smoking, who addressed the elder by a military title, and began a slangy conversation with him upon the great New Haven subject,—boat-racing. About eleven, three or four other young men came in, to whom cigars were furnished by the military chieftain. All together they blew a very respectable cloud, and the conversation, being so strongly reinforced, became more animated. Boating was still the principal theme. The singular merits of Pittsburg oars were discussed. A warm dispute arose as to who was the builder of a certain boat that had won a race three years ago. Much admiration was expressed for the muscle, the nerve, and, above all, for the style and method, of the crew of the Harvard boat, which had beaten the Yale boat a few weeks before.

Nevertheless, it did not occur to me that these smoking and damning gentlemen could be members of the college. I supposed they were young loafers of the town, who took an interest in the pleasures of the students, and were exchanging opinions thereon with their natural chief, the lord of the stable. At length one said to another, "Will Jones be here this week?" The reply was: "No, I wrote to the fellow; but, damn him, he says he can't get here till next Thursday." "Why, what's the matter with the cuss?" "O, he's had the fever and ague, and he says there's no pull in him." This led me to suspect that these young fellows were the envied youths of whom I had been dreaming under the elms, — a suspicion which the subsequent conversation soon confirmed. There was nothing wrong or harmful in the subject of their talk. The remarkable circumstance was, that all the difference which naturally exists, and naturally appears, between an educated and an uneducated person was obliterated; and it seemed, too, that the smoke was the "common element" in which the two were blended. It was the *cigar* that kept the students there talking boat till midnight with an elderly ignoramus, and it was the cigar that was always drawing them down to his level. If he had not handed round his cigar-case, they would have exhausted all the natural interest of the subject in a few minutes, and gone home to bed. All of them, too, as it happened, confessed that smoking lessens the power of a man to row a boat, and lamented that a certain student would be lost to the crack crew from his unwillingness to give up his pipe.

Smoking lures and detains men from the society of ladies. This herding of men into clubs, these dinners to which men only are invited, the late sitting at the table after the ladies have withdrawn, the gathering of male guests into some smoking-room, apart from the ladies of the party, — is not the cigar chiefly responsible for these atrocities? Men are not society; women are not society: society is the mingling of the two sexes in such a way that each restrains and inspires the other. That community is already far gone in degeneracy in which men prefer to band together by themselves, in which men do not crave the society of ladies, and value it as the chief charm of existence. "What is the real attraction of these gorgeous establishments?" I asked, the other evening, of an acquaintance who was about to enter one of the new club-houses on Fifth Avenue. His reply was: "No women can enter them! Once within these sacred walls, we are safe from everything that wears a petticoat!" Are we getting to be Turks? The Turks shut women in; we shut them out. The Turks build harems for their women; but we find it necessary to abandon to women our abodes, and construct harems for ourselves.

Humiliating as the truth is, it must be confessed, tobacco is woman's rival, her successful rival. It is the cigar and the pipe (it used to be wine and punch) that enable men to endure one another during the whole of a long evening. Remove from every clubhouse all the means of intoxication, — i. e. all the wine and **tobacco,** — and seven out of every ten of them would cease to exist in one year. Men would come together for a few evenings, as usual, talk over the evening papers, yawn and go away, perhaps go home, — a place which our confirmed clubbists only know as a convenience for sleeping and breakfasting. One of the worst effects of smoking **is** that it deadens our susceptibility to tedium, and enables us to keep on enduring what we ought to war against and overcome. It is drunken people who "won't go home till morning." Tyrants and oppressors are wrong in drawing so much revenue from tobacco; they ought rather to give it away, for it tends to enable people to sit down content under every kind of oppression.

Men say, in reply to those who object to their clubs, their men's dinner-parties, and their smoking-rooms: "Women overwhelm society with superfluous dry goods. The moment ladies are invited, the whole affair becomes a mere question of costume. A party at which ladies assist is little more than an exhibition of wearing apparel. They dress, too, not for the purpose of giving pleasure to men, but for the purpose of inflicting pain on one another. Besides, a lady who is carrying a considerable estate upon her person must devote a great part of her attention to the management of that estate. She **may be** talking to Mr. Smith about Shakespeare and the musical-glasses, but the thing her mind is really intent upon is crushing Mrs. Smith with her new lace. Even dancing is nothing but an exceedingly laborious and anxious wielding of yards of silk trailing out behind!" etc.

Smoky diners-out will recognize this line of remark. When ladies have left the table, and are amusing themselves in the drawing-room in ways which may sometimes be trivial, but are never sensual, men frequently fall into discourse, over their cigars, upon the foibles of the sex, and often succeed in delivering themselves of one or more of the observations just quoted. As these noble critics sit boozing and smoking, they can sometimes hear the brilliant run upon the piano, or the notes of a finely trained voice, or the joyous laughter of a group of girls, — all inviting them to a higher and purer enjoyment than steeping their senses in barbarous smoke. But they stick to their cigars, and assume a lofty moral superiority over the lovely beings, the evidence of whose better civilization is sounding in their ears.

Now, one of the subtle, mysterious effects of tobacco upon "the male of our species" is to disenchant him with regard to the female. It makes us read the poem entitled Woman as though it were only a piece of prose. It takes off the edge of virility. If it does not make a man less masculine, it keeps his masculinity in a state of partial torpor, which causes him to look upon women, not indeed without a certain curiosity, but without enthusiasm, without romantic elevation of mind, without any feeling of awe and veneration for the august Mothers of our race. It tends to make us regard women from what we may style the Black

Crook point of view. The young man who boasted that he had seen **the Black** Crook forty-seven times in three months must have been an irreclaimable smoker. Nothing but the dulled, sensualized masculinity caused by this peculiar poison could have blinded men to the ghastly and haggard ugliness of that exhibition. The pinched and painted vacancy of those poor girls' faces; the bony horrors of some of their necks, and **the** flabby redundancy of others; the cheap and tawdry splendors; the stale, rejected tricks of London pantomimes; three **or four tons of** unhappy girls suspended in the air in various agonizing attitudes, — to think that such a show could have run for seventeen months! Even if science did not justify the conjecture, I should **be** disposed, for the honor of human nature, **to lay the** blame of all this upon tobacco.

To a man who is uncorrupt **and** properly constituted, woman remains always something of a mystery and a romance. He never interprets her quite literally. She, on her part, is always striving to remain a poem, and is never weary of bringing out new editions of herself in novel bindings. Not till she has been utterly conquered and crushed by hopeless misery or a false religion does she give up the dream of still being a pleasant enchantment. To this end, without precisely knowing why, she turns the old dress, retrims it, or arrays **herself in** the freshness of a new one, ever striving to **present** herself in recreated loveliness. Uncontaminated **man** sympathizes with this intention, **and** easily lends himself to the renewed charm. Have you not felt something of this, old smokers, when, after indulging in the stock jests and sneers at womankind, you lay aside your cigars, and "join the ladies," arrayed in bright colors and bewitching novelties of dress, moving gracefully in the brilliant gas-light, or arranged in glowing groups about the room? Has not the truth flashed upon you, at such moments, that you had been talking prose upon a subject essentially poetical? Have you never felt how mean and low a thing it was to linger in sensual stupefaction, rather than take your proper place in such a scene as this?

It is true, that a few women in commercial cities, — a few bankers' and brokers' wives, and others, — bewildered by the possession of new wealth, do go to ridiculous excess in dressing, and thus bring reproach upon the art. It were well if their husbands did no worse. Now and then, too, is presented the melancholy spectacle of an extravagant hussy marring, perhaps spoiling, the career of her husband by tasteless and unprincipled expenditures in the decoration of her person. But is it wholly her fault? Is he not the purse-holder? Is it not a husband's duty to prevent his wife from dishonoring herself in that manner? When men are sensual, women will be frivolous. When men abandon their homes and all the noble pleasures of society in order to herd together in clubs and smoking-rooms, what right have they to object if the ladies amuse themselves in the only innocent way accessible to them? The wonder is that they confine themselves to the innocent delights of the toilet. A husband who spends one day and seven evenings of every week at his club ought to expect that his wife will provide herself both with fine clothes and some one who will admire them. Besides, for one woman who shocks us by wasting upon her person an undue part of the family resources, there are ten who astonish us by the delightful results which their taste and ingenuity contrive out of next to nothing.

It would be absurd to say that smoking is the cause of evils which originate in the weakness and imperfection of human nature. The point is simply this: tobacco, by disturbing and impairing virility, tends to vitiate the relations between the sexes, tends to lessen man's interest in women and his enjoyment of their society, and enables him to endure and be contented with, and finally even to prefer, the companionship of men. And this is the true reason why almost every lady of spirit is the irreconcilable foe of tobacco. It is not merely that she dislikes the stale odor of the smoke in her curtains, nor merely that her quick eye discerns its hostility to health and life. These things would make her disapprove the weed. But instinct causes her dimly to perceive that this ridiculous brown leaf is the rival of her sex. Women do not disapprove their rivals; they hate them.

Smoking certainly does blunt a man's sense of cleanliness. It certainly is an unclean habit. Does the reader remember the fine scene in "Shirley," in which the lover soliloquizes in Shirley's own boudoir, just after that "stainless virgin" has gone out? She had gone away suddenly, it appears, and left disorder behind her; but every object bore upon it the legible inscription, *I belong to a lady!* "Nothing sordid, nothing soiled," says Louis Moore. "Look at the pure kid of this little glove, at the fresh, unsullied satin of the bag." This is one of those happy touches of the great artist which convey more meaning than whole paint-pots of common coloring. What a pleasing sense it gives us of the sweet cleanness of the high-bred maiden! If smokers were to be judged by the places they have *left*, — by the smoking-car after a long day's use, by the dinner-table at which they have sat late, by the bachelor's quarters when the bachelor has gone down town, — they must be rated very low in the scale of civilization.

We must admit, too, I think, that smoking dulls a man's sense of the rights of others. Horace Greeley is accustomed to sum up his opinion upon this branch of the subject by saying: "When a man begins to smoke, he immediately becomes a hog." He probably uses the word "hog" in two senses: namely, *hog*, an unclean creature; and *hog*, a creature devoid of a correct sense of what is due to other creatures. "Go into a public gathering," he has written, "where a speaker of delicate lungs, with an invincible repulsion to tobacco, is trying to discuss some important topic so that a thousand men can hear and understand him, yet whereinto ten or twenty smokers have introduced themselves, a long-nine projecting horizontally from beneath the nose of each, a fire at one end and a fool at the other, and mark how the puff, puffing gradually transforms the atmosphere (none too pure at best) into that of some foul and pestilential cavern, choking the utterance of the speaker, and distracting (by annoyance) the attention of the hearers, until the argument is arrested or its effect utterly destroyed." If these men, he adds, are not blackguards, who are blackguards? He mitigates the severity of this conclusion, however, by telling an anecdote: "Brethren," said Parson Strong, of Hartford, preaching a Connecticut election sermon, in high party times, some fifty years ago, "it has been charged that I have said every Democrat is a horse-thief; I never did. What I *did* say was only that every horse-thief is a Democrat, and *that* I can prove." Mr. Greeley challenges the universe to produce a genuine blackguard who is not a lover of the weed in some of its forms, and promises to reward the finder with the gift of two white blackbirds.

Mr. Greeley exaggerates. Some of the best gentlemen alive smoke, and some of the dirtiest blackguards do not; but most intelligent smokers are conscious that the practice, besides being in itself unclean, dulls the smoker's sense of cleanliness, and, what is still worse, dulls his sense of what is due to others, and especially of what is due to the presence of ladies.

The cost of tobacco ought perhaps to be considered before we conclude whether or not it pays to smoke; since every man who smokes, not only pays his share of the whole expense of the weed to mankind, but he also supports and justifies mankind in incurring that expense. The statistics of tobacco are tremendous, even to the point of being incredible. It is gravely asserted, in Messrs. Ripley and Dana's excellent and most trustworthy Cyclopædia, that the consumption of cigars in Cuba — the mere consumption — amounts to ten cigars per day for every man, woman, and child on the island. Besides this, Cuba exports two billions of cigars a year, which vary in price from twenty cents each (in gold) to two cents. In the manufacture of Manilla cheroots, — a small item in the trade, — the labor of seven thousand men and twelve hundred women is absorbed. Holland, where much of the tobacco used in smoky Germany is manufactured, employs, it is said, one million pale people in the business. In Bremen there are four thousand pallid or yellow cigar-makers. In the United States the weed exhausts four hundred thousand acres of excellent land, and employs forty thousand sickly and cadaverous cigar and tobacco makers. In England, where there is a duty upon tobacco of seventy-five cents a pound, and upon cigars of nearly four dollars a pound, the government derives about six million pounds sterling every year from tobacco. The French government gets from its monopoly of the tobacco trade nearly two hundred million francs per annum, and Austria over eighty million francs. It is computed that the world is now producing one thousand million pounds of tobacco every year, at a *total* cost of five hundred millions of dollars. To this must be added the cost of pipes, and a long catalogue of smoking conveniences and accessories.

In the London Exhibition there were four amber mouth-pieces, valued at two hundred and fifty guineas each. A plain, small, serviceable meerschaum pipe now costs in New York seven dollars, and the prices rise from that sum to a thousand dollars; but where is the young man who does not possess one? We have in New York two (perhaps more) extensive manufactories of these pipes; and very interesting it is to look in at the windows and inspect the novelties in this branch of art? In Vienna men earn their living (and their dying too) by smoking meerschaums for the purpose of starting the process of "coloring." Happily, the high price of labor has hitherto prevented the introduction of this industry into America.

An inhabitant of the United States who smokes a pipe only, and good tobacco in that pipe, can now get his smoking for twenty-five dollars a year. One who smokes good cigars freely (say ten a day at twenty cents each) must expend between seven and eight hundred dollars a year. Almost every one whose eye may chance to fall upon these lines will be able to mention at least one man whose smoking costs him several hundred dollars per annum, — from three hundred to twelve hundred. On the other hand, our friend the hod-carrier can smoke a whole week upon ten cents' worth of tobacco, and buy a pipe for two cents which he can smoke till it is black with years.

All this inconceivable expenditure — this five hundred millions per annum — comes out of the world's surplus, that precious fund which must pay all the cost, both of improving and extending civilization. Knowledge, art, literature, have to be supported out of what is left after food, clothes, fire, shelter, and defence have all been paid for. If the surest test of civilization, whether of an individual or of a community, is the use made of surplus revenue, what can we say of the civilization of a race that expends five hundred millions of dollars every year for an indulgence which is nearly an unmitigated injury? The surplus revenue, too, of every community is very small; for nearly the whole force of human nature is expended necessarily in the unending struggle for life. The most prosperous, industrious, economical, and civilized community that now exists in the world, or that ever existed, is, perhaps, the Commonwealth of Massachusetts. Yes, take it for all in all, Massachusetts, imperfect as it is, is about the best thing man has yet done in the way of a commonwealth. And yet the surplus revenue of Massachusetts is set down at only three cents a day for each inhabitant; and out of this the community has to pay for its knowledge, decoration, and luxury. Man, it must be confessed, after having been in business for so many thousands of years, is still in very narrow circumstances, and most assuredly cannot afford to spend five hundred millions a year in an injurious physical indulgence.

It is melancholy to observe what a small, mean, precarious, grudging support we give to the best things, if they are of the kind which must be sustained out of our surplus. At Cambridge the other day, while looking about among the ancient barracks in which the students live, I had the curiosity to ask concerning the salaries of the professors in Harvard College,— supposing, of course, that such learned and eminent persons received a compensation proportioned to the dignity of their offices, the importance of their labors, and the celebrity of their names. Alas! it is not so. A good reporter on the New York press gets just about as much money as the President of the College, and the professors receive such salaries as fifteen and eighteen hundred dollars a year. The very gifts of inconsiderate benefactors have impoverished the college, few of whom, it seems, have been able to give money to the institution; most of them have merely *bought* distinction from it. Thus professorships in plenty have been endowed and *named;* but the college is hampered, and its resources have become insufficient, by being divided among a multitude of objects. I beg the reader, the next time he gives Harvard University a hundred thousand dollars, or leaves it a million in his will, to make the sum a *gift,*—a gift to the trustees,— to be expended as *they* deem best for the general and permanent good of the institution, and not to neutralize the benefit of the donation by conditions dictated by vanity. Yale, I have since learned, is no better off. At all our colleges, it seems, the professors either starve upon twelve or fifteen hundred dollars a year, or eke out a subsistence by taking pupils, or by some other arduous extra labor. But what wonder that learning pines, when we every year waste millions upon millions of the fund out of which **alone learning** can be supported!

It is so with all high **and** spiritual things. How the theatre languishes! There **are but** four cities in the United States where a good **and** complete theatre could be sustained. In the great **and** wealthy city of New York there **has** never been **more** than one at a time, nor **always one.** How **small, too,** the sale of good books, even those of a popular cast! **One** of the most interesting works **ever** published in **the United States is** the " Life of Josiah Quincy," by **his** son Edmund Quincy. It **is not** an abstruse production. **The** narrative is easy and flowing, interspersed with welltold anecdotes **of** celebrated men, — Washington, **Lafayette, John Adams, John** Randolph, Hancock, Jefferson, **and** many others. **Above** all, the book exhibits **and** interprets, in the **most** agreeable **manner, a** triumphant human life; showing how **it came to pass that Josiah** Quincy, in this perplexing **and** perilous **world,** was **able to** live happily, healthily, honorably, **and** usefully **for** ninety-three years! Splendid triumph **of** civilization! Ninety-three years of joyous, dignified, and beneficial existence! One would have thought that many thousands **of** people **in** the United States would have hurried to their several bookstores to bear away, rejoicing, **a volume recounting** such **a marvel,** the explanation **of** which **so** nearly concerns **us all.** The book **has now** been published three **months or** more, and **has not yet** sold more than **three thousand** copies! **Young men cannot** waste **their hard-earned** money upon a **three-dollar book.** It is the price of a bundle of cigars!

Mr. **Henry** Ward Beecher has recently told us, in one of his "Ledger" articles, how he earned his first ten dollars, and what he did with it. While he was a student in Amherst he was invited to deliver a Fourth-of-July temperance address in Brattleboro', forty miles distant. His travelling expenses were to be paid; but the brilliant scheme occurred to him to walk the eighty miles, and earn the stage fare by saving it. He did so, and received by mail after his return a ten-dollar bill, — the first ten dollars he had ever possessed, and the first money he had ever earned. He instantly gave a proof that the test of a person's civilization is the use he makes of his surplus money. He spent the whole of it upon an edition of the works of Edmund Burke, and carried the volumes to his room, a happy youth. It was not the best choice, in literature, perhaps; but it was one that marked the civilized being, and indicated the future instructor of his species. Suppose he had invested the sum (and we all know students who would make just that use of an unexpected ten-dollar bill) in a new meerschaum and a bag of Lone-Jack tobacco! At the end of his college course he would have had, probably, a finely colored pipe, — perhaps the prettiest pipe of his year; but he would not have had that little "library of fifty volumes," the solace of his coming years of poverty and fever and ague, always doing their part toward expanding him from a sectarian into a man of the world, and lifting him from the slavery of a mean country parish toward the mastership of a metropolitan congregation. His was the very nature to have been quenched by tobacco. If he had bought a pipe that day, instead of books, he might be at this moment a petty D.D., preaching safe inanity or silly eccentricity in some obscure corner of the world, and going to Europe every five years for his health.

We all perceive that smoking has made bold and rapid encroachments of late years. It is said that the absurdly situated young man who passes in the world by the undescriptive name of the Prince of Wales smokes in drawing-rooms in the presence of ladies. This tale is probably false; scandalous tales respecting conspicuous persons are so generally false, that it is always safest and fairest to reject them as a matter of course, unless they rest upon testimony that ought to convince a jury. Nevertheless, it is true that smoke is creeping toward the drawing-room, and rolls in clouds where once it would not have dared to send a whiff. One reason of this is, that the cigar, and the pipe too, have "got into literature," where they shed abroad a most alluring odor. That passage, for example, in "Jane Eyre," where the timid, anxious Jane, returning after an absence, scents Rochester's cigar before she catches sight of his person, is enough to make any old smoker feel for his cigar-case; and all through the book smoke plays a dignified and attractive part. Mr. Rochester's cigars, we feel, must be of excellent quality (thirty cents each, at least); we see how freely they burn; we smell their delicious fragrance. Charlotte Brontë was, perhaps, one of the few women who have a morbid love of the odor of tobacco, who crave its stimulating aid as men do; and therefore her Rochester has a fragrance of the weed about him at all times, with which many readers have been captivated. "Jane Eyre" is the book of recent years which has been most frequently imitated, and consequently the circulating libraries are populous with smoking heroes. Byron, Thackeray, and many other popular authors have written passages in which the smoke of tobacco insinuates itself most agreeably into the reader's gentle senses.

Many smokers, too, have been made such by the unexplained rigor with which the practice is sometimes forbidden. Forbidden it must be in all schools; but merely forbidding it and making it a dire offence will not suffice in these times. Some of the most pitiable slaves of smoke I have ever known were brought up in families and schools where smoking was invested with the irresistible charm of being the worst thing a boy could do, except running away. Deep in the heart of the woods, high up in rocky hills, far from the haunts of men and schoolmasters (not to speak of places less salubrious), boys assemble on holiday afternoons to sicken themselves with furtive smoke, returning at the close of the day to relate the dazzling exploit to their companions. In this way the habit sometimes becomes so tyrannical, that, if the victims of it should give a sincere definition of "vacation," it would be this, "The time when boys can get a chance to smoke every day." I can also state, that the only school I ever knew or heard of in which young men who had formed the habit were induced to break themselves of it was the only school I ever knew or heard of in which all students above the age of sixteen were allowed to smoke. Still, it *must* be forbidden. Professor Charlier, of New York, will not have in his school a boy who smokes even at home in his father's presence, or in the street; and he is right; but it requires all his talents as a disciplinarian and all his influence as a member of society to enforce the rule. Nor would even his vigilance avail if he confined himself to the cold enunciation of the law: Thou shalt not smoke.

To forbid young men to smoke, without making an honest and earnest and skilful attempt to convince their understandings that the practice is pernicious, is sometimes followed by deplorable consequences. At the Naval Academy at Annapolis, not only is smoking forbidden, but the prohibition is effectual. There are four hundred young men confined within walls, and subjected to such discipline that it is impossible for a rule to be broken, the breaking of which betrays itself. The result is, that nearly all the students chew tobacco,—many of them to very great excess, and to their most serious and manifest injury. That great national institution teems with abuses, but, perhaps, all the other deleterious influences of the place united do less harm than this one abomination.

On looking over the articles upon tobacco in the Encyclopædias, we occasionally find writers declaring or conjecturing that, as smoking has become a habit almost universal, there must be, in the nature of things, a reason which accounts for and justifies it. Accounts for it, *yes;* justifies it, *no.*

So long as man lives the life of a pure savage, he has good health without ever bestowing a thought upon the matter. Nature, like a good farmer, saves the best for seed. The mightiest bull becomes the father of the herd; the great warrior, the great hunter, has the most wives and children. The sickly children are destroyed by the hardships of savage life, and those who survive are compelled to put forth such exertions in procuring food and defending their wigwams that they are always "in training." The pure savage has not the skill nor the time to extract from the wilds in which he lives the poisons that could deprave his taste and impair his vigor. Your Indian sleeps, with scanty covering, in a wigwam that freely admits the air. In his own way, he is an exquisite cook. Neither Delmonico nor Parker nor Professor Blot ever cooked a salmon or a partridge as well as a Rocky Mountain Indian cooks them; and when he has cooked his fish or his bird, he eats with it some perfectly simple preparation of Indian corn. He is an absolutely *unstimulated* animal. The natural working of his internal machinery generates all the vital force he wants. He is as healthy as a buffalo, as a prize-fighter, as the stroke-oar of a university boat.

But in our civilized, sedentary life, he who would have good health must fight for it. Many people have the insolence to become parents who have no right to aspire to that dignity; children are born who have no right to exist; and skill preserves many whom nature is eager to destroy. Civilized man, too, has learned the trick of heading off some of the diseases that used to sweep over whole regions of the earth, and lay low the weakliest tenth of the population. Consequently, while the average duration of human life has been increased, the average tone of human health has been lowered. Fewer die, and fewer are quite well. Very many of us breathe vitiated air, and keep nine tenths of the body quiescent for twenty-two or twenty-three hours out of every twenty-four. Immense numbers cherish gloomy, depressing opinions, and convert the day set apart for rest and recreation into one which aggravates some of the worst tendencies of the week, and counteracts none of them. Half the population of the United States violate the laws of nature every time they take sustenance; and the children go, crammed with indigestion, to sit six hours in hot, ill-ventilated or unventilated school-rooms. Except in a few large towns, the bread and meat are almost universally inferior or bad; and the only viands that are good are those which ought not to be eaten at all. At most family tables, after a course of meat which has the curious property of being both soft and tough, a wild profusion of ingenious puddings, pies, cakes, and other abominable trash, beguiles the young, disgusts the mature, and injures all. From bodies thus imperfectly nourished, we demand excessive exertions of all kinds.

Hence, the universal craving for artificial aids to digestion. Hence, the universal use of stimulants,— whiskey, Worcestershire sauce, beer, wine, coffee, tea, tobacco. This is the only reason I can discover in the nature of things here for the widespread, increasing propensity to smoke. As all the virtues are akin, and give loyal aid to one another, so are all the vices in alliance, and play into one another's hands. Many a smoker will discover, when at last he breaks the bond of his servitude, that his pipe, trifling a matter as it may seem to him now, was really the power that kept down his whole nature, and vulgarized his whole existence. In many instances the single act of self-control involved in giving up the habit would necessitate and include a complete regeneration, first physical, then moral.

Whether the Coming Man will drink wine or be a teetotaller has not yet, perhaps, been positively ascertained; but it is certain he will not smoke. Nothing can be surer than that. The Coming Man will be as healthy as Tecumseh, as clean as Shirley, and as well groomed as Dexter. He will not fly the female of his species, nor wall himself in from her approach, nor give her cause to prefer his absence. We are not left to infer or conjecture this; we can ascertain it from what we know of the messengers who have announced the coming of the Coming Man. The most distinguished of these was Goethe, — perhaps the nearest approach to the complete human being that has yet appeared. The mere fact that this admirable person lived always unpolluted by this seductive poison is a fact of some significance; but the important fact is, that he *could not* have smoked and remained Goethe. When we get close to the man, and live intimately with him, we perceive the impossibility of his ever having been a smoker. We can as easily fancy Desdemona smoking a cigarette as the highly groomed, alert, refined, imperial Goethe with a cigar in his mouth. In America, the best gentleman and most variously learned and accomplished man we have had — the man, too, who had in him most of what will constitute the glory of the future — was Thomas Jefferson, Democrat, of Virginia. He was versed in six langauges; he danced, rode, and hunted as well as General Washington; he played the violin well, wrote admirably, farmed skilfully, and was a most generous, affectionate, humane, and great-souled human being. It was the destiny of this ornament and consolation of his species to raise tobacco, and live by tobacco all his life. But he knew too much to use it himself; or, to speak more correctly, his fine feminine senses, his fine masculine instincts, revolted from the use of it, without any assistance from his understanding.

There is no trace of the pipe in the writings of Washington or Franklin; probably they never smoked; so that we may rank the three great men of America — Washington, Franklin, and Jefferson — among the exempts. Washington Irving, who was the first literary man of the United States to achieve a universal reputation, and who is still regarded as standing at the head of our literature, was no smoker. Two noted Americans, Dr. Nott and John Quincy Adams, after having been slaves of the weed for many years, escaped from bondage and smoked no more. These distinguished names may serve as a set-off to the list of illustrious smokers previously given.

Among the nations of the earth most universally addicted to smoking are the Turks, the Persians, the Chinese, the Spanish, — all slaves of tradition, submissive to tyrants, unenterprising, averse to improvement, despisers of women. Next to these, perhaps, we must place the Germans, a noble race, renowned for two thousand years for the masculine vigor of the men and the motherly dignity of the women. Smoking is a blight upon this valuable breed of men; it steals away from their minds much of the alertness and decision that naturally belong to such minds as they have, and it impairs their bodily health. Go, on some festive day, to "Jones's Woods," where you may sometimes see five thousand Germans — men, women, and children — amusing themselves in their simple and rational way. Not one face in ten has the clear, bright look of health. Nearly all the faces have a certain tallowy aspect, — yellowish in color, with a dull shine upon them. You perceive plainly that it is not well with these good people; they are not conforming to nature's requirements; they are not the Germans of

Tacitus, — ruddy, tough, happy, and indomitable. To lay the whole blame of this decline upon smoking, which is only one of many bad habits of theirs, would be absurd. What I insist upon is this: Smoking, besides doing its part toward lowering the tone of the bodily health, deadens our sense of other physical evils, and makes us submit to them more patiently. If our excellent German fellow-citizens were to throw away their pipes, they would speedily toss their cast-iron sausages after them, and become more fastidious in the choice of air for their own and their children's breathing, and reduce their daily allowance of lager-bier. Their first step toward physical regeneration will be, must be, the suppression of the pipe.

One hopeful sign for the future is, that this great subject of the physical aids and the physical obstacles to virtue is attracting attention and rising into importance. Our philanthropists have stopped giving tracts to hungry people; at least they give bread first. It is now a recognized truth, that it takes a certain number of cubic yards for a person to be virtuous in; and that, consequently, in that square mile of New York in which two hundred and ninety thousand people live, there must be — absolutely *must* be — an immense number of unvirtuous persons. No human virtue or civilization can long exist where four families live in a room, some of whom take boarders. The way to regenerate this New York mile is simply to widen Manhattan Island by building three bridges over the East

River, and to shorten the island by making three lines of underground or overground railroad to the upper end of it. We may say, too, there are circles — not many, it is true, but some — in which a man's religion would not be considered a very valuable acquisition, if, when he had "got" it, he kept on chewing tobacco. Such a flagrant and abominable violation of the Creator's laws, by a person distinctly professing a special veneration for them, would be ludicrous, if it were not so pernicious.

The time is at hand when these simple and fundamental matters will have their proper place in all our schemes for the improvement of one another. The impulse in this direction given by the publication of the most valuable work of this century — Buckle's "History of Civilization in England" — will not expend itself in vain. If that author had but lived, he would not have disdained, in recounting the obstacles to civilization, to consider the effects upon the best modern brains of a poison that lulls their noblest faculties to torpor, and enables them languidly to endure what they ought constantly to fight.

It is not difficult to stop smoking, except for one class of smokers, — those whom it has radically injured, and whose lives it is shortening. For all such the discontinuance of the practice will be almost as difficult as it is desirable. No rule can be given which will apply to all or to many such cases; but each man must fight it out on the line he finds best, and must not be surprised if it takes him a great deal longer than "all summer." If one of this class of smokers should gain deliverance from his bondage after a two years' struggle, he would be doing well. A man who had been smoking twenty cigars a day for several years, and should suddenly stop, would be almost certain either to relapse or fall into some worse habit, — chewing, whiskey, or opium. Perhaps his best way would be to put himself upon half allowance for a year, and devote the second year to completing his cure, — always taking care to live in other respects more wisely and temperately, and thus lessen the craving for a stimulant. The more smoke is hurting a man, the harder it is for him to stop smoking; and almost all whom the practice is destroying rest under the delusion that they could stop without the least effort, if they liked.

The vast majority of smokers — seven out of every ten, at least — can, without the least danger or much inconvenience, cease smoking at once, totally and forever.

As I have now given a trial to both sides of the question, I beg respectfully to assure the brotherhood of smokers that it does *not* pay to smoke. It really does not. I can work better and longer than before. I have less headache. I have a better opinion of myself. I enjoy exercise more, and step out much more vigorously. My room is cleaner. The bad air of our theatres and other public places disgusts and infuriates me more, but exhausts me less. I think I am rather better tempered, as well as more cheerful and satisfied.

I endure the inevitable ills of life with more fortitude, and look forward more hopefully to the coming years. It did not pay to smoke, but, most decidedly, it pays to stop smoking.

DRINKING.

WILL THE COMING MAN DRINK WINE?

THE teetotalers confess their failure. After forty-five years of zealous and well-meant effort in the "cause," they agree that people are drinking more than ever. Dr. R. T. Trall of New York, the most thoroughgoing teetotalar extant, exclaims: "Where are we to-day? Defeated on all sides. The enemy victorious and rampant everywhere. More intoxicating liquors manufactured and drunk than ever before. Why is this?" Why, indeed! When the teetotalers can answer that question correctly, they will be in a fair way to gain upon the "enemy" that is now so "rampant." They are not the first people who have mistaken a symptom of disease for the disease itself, and striven to cure a cancer by applying salve and plaster and cooling washes to the sore. They are not the first travellers through this Wilderness who have tried to extinguish a smouldering fire, and discovered, at last, that they had been pouring water into the crater of a volcano.

Dr. Trall thinks we should all become teetotalers very soon, if only the doctors would stop prescribing wine, beer, and whiskey to their patients. But the doctors will not. They like a glass of wine themselves. Dr. Trall tells us that, during the Medical Convention held at St. Louis a few years ago, the doctors dined together, and upon the table were "forty kinds of alcoholic liquors." The most enormous feed ever accomplished under a roof in America, I suppose, was the great dinner of the doctors, given in New York, fifteen years ago, at the Metropolitan Hall. I had the pleasure on that occasion of seeing half an acre of doctors all eating and drinking at once, and I can testify that very few of them — indeed, none that I could discover — neglected the bottle. It was an occasion which united all the established barbarisms of a public dinner, — absence of ladies, indigestible food in most indigestible quantities, profuse and miscellaneous drinking, clouds of smoke, late sitting, and wild speaking. Why not? Do not these men live and thrive upon such practices? Why should they not set an example of the follies which enrich them? It is only heroes who offend, deny, and rebuke the people upon whose favor their fortune depends; and there are never many heroes in the world at one time. No, no, Dr. Trall! the doctors are good fellows; but their affair is to cure disease, not to preserve health.

One man, it seems, and only one, has had much success in dissuading people from drinking, and that was Father Mathew. A considerable proportion of his converts in Ireland, it is said, remain faithful to their pledge; and most of the Catholic parishes in the United States have a Father Mathew Society connected with them, which is both a teetotal and a mutual-benefit organization. In New York and adjacent cities the number of persons belonging to such societies is about twenty-seven thousand. On the anniversary of Father Mathew's birth they walk in procession, wearing aprons, carrying large banners (when the wind permits), and heaping up gayly dressed children into pryamids and mountains drawn by six and eight horses. At their weekly or monthly meetings they sing songs, recite poetry, perform plays and farces, enact comic characters, and, in other innocent ways, endeavor to convince on-lookers that people can be happy and merry, uproariously merry, without putting a headache between their teeth. These societies seem to be a great and unmingled good. They do actually help poor men to withstand their only American enemy. They have, also, the approval of the most inveterate drinkers, both Catholic and Protestant. Jones complacently remarks, as he gracefully sips his claret (six dollars per dozen) that this total abstinence, you know, is an excellent thing for emigrants; to which Brown and Robinson invariably assent.

Father Mathew used to administer his pledge to people who *knelt* before him, and when they had taken it he made over them the sign of the cross. He did not usually deliver addresses; he did not relate amusing anecdotes; he did not argue the matter; he merely pronounced the pledge, and gave to it the sanction of religion, and something of the solemnity of a sacrament. The present Father Mathew Societies are also closely connected with the church, and the pledge is regarded by the members as of religious obligation. Hence, these societies are successful, in a respectable degree; and we may look, with the utmost confidence, to see them extend and flourish until a great multitude of Catholics are teetotalers. Catholic priests, I am informed, generally drink wine, and very many of them smoke; but *they* are able to induce men to take the pledge without setting them an example of abstinence, just as parents sometimes deny their children pernicious viands of which they freely partake themselves.

But *we* cannot proceed in that way. Our religion has not power to control a physical craving by its mere fiat, nor do we all yet perceive what a deadly and shameful sin it is to vitiate our own bodies. The Catholic Church is antiquity. The Catholic Church is childhood. *We* are living in modern times; *we* have grown a little past childhood; and when we are asked to relinquish a pleasure, we demand to be convinced that it is best we should. By and by we shall all comprehend that, when a person means to reform his life, the very first thing for him to do — the thing preliminary and most indispensable — will be to cease violating physical laws. The time, I hope, is at hand, when an audience in a theatre, who catch a manager cheating them out of their fair allowance of fresh air, will not sit and gasp, and inhale destruction till eleven P. M., and then rush wildly to the street for relief. They will stop the play; they will tear up the benches, if necessary; they will throw things on the stage; they will knock a hole in the wall; they will *have* the means of breathing, or perish in the struggle. But at present people do not know what they are doing when they inhale poison. They do not know that more than one half of all the diseases that plague us most — scarlet fever, small-pox, measles, and all the worst fevers — come of breathing bad air. Not a child last winter would have had the scarlet fever, if all the children in the world had slept with a window open, and had had pure air to breathe all day. This is Miss Nightingale's opinion, and there is no better authority. People are ignorant of these things, and they are therefore indifferent to them. They will remain indifferent till they are enlightened.

Our teetotal friends have not neglected the scientific questions involved in their subject; nor have they settled them. Instead of insulting the public intelligence by asserting that the wines mentioned in the Bible were some kind of unintoxicating slop, and exasperating the public temper by premature prohibitory laws, they had better expend their strength upon the science of the matter, and prove to mankind, if they can, that these agreeable drinks which they denounce are really hurtful. We all know that excess is hurtful. We also know that adulterated liquors may be. But is the thing in itself pernicious? — pure wine taken in moderation? good beer? genuine Old Bourbon?

For one, I wish it could be demonstrated that these things are hurtful. Sweeping, universal truths are as convenient as they are rare. The evils resulting from excess in drinking are so enormous and so terrible, that it would be a relief to know that alcoholic liquors are in themselves evil, and to be always avoided. What are the romantic woes of a Desdemona, or the brief picturesque sorrows of a Lear, compared with the thirty years' horror and desolation caused by a drunken parent? We laugh when we read Lamb's funny description of his waking up in the morning, and learning in what condition he had come home the night before by seeing all his clothes carefully folded. But his sister Mary did not laugh at it. He was all she had; it was tragedy to her, — this self-destruction of her sole stay and consolation. Goethe did not find it a laughing matter to have a drunken wife in his house for fifteen years, nor a jest to have his son brought in drunk from the tavern, and to see him dead in his coffin, the early victim of champagne. Who would not *like* to have a clear conviction, that what we have to do with regard to all such fluids is to let them alone? I am sure I should. It is a great advantage to have your enemy in plain sight, and to be sure he *is* an enemy.

What is wine? Chemists tell us they do not know. Three fifths of a glass of wine is water. One fifth is alcohol. Of the remaining fifth, about one half is sugar. One tenth of the whole quantity remains to be accounted for. A small part of that tenth is the acid which makes vinegar sour. Water, alcohol, sugar, acid, — these make very nearly the whole body of the wine; but if we mix these things in the proportions in which they are found in Madeira, the liquid is a disgusting mess, nothing like Madeira. The great chemists confess they do not know what that last small fraction of the glass of wine is, upon which its flavor, its odor, its fascination, depend. They do not know what it is that makes the difference between port and sherry, but are obliged to content themselves with giving it a hard name.

Similar things are admitted concerning the various kinds of spirituous and malt liquors. Chemistry seems to agree with the temperance society, that wine, beer, brandy, gin, whiskey, and rum are alcohol and water, mixed in different proportions, and with some slight differences of flavoring and coloring matter. In all these drinks, teetotalers maintain, *alcohol is* **power**, the other ingredients being mere dilution and flavoring. Wine, they assure us, is alcohol and water flavored with grapes; beer is alcohol and water flavored with malt and hops; Bourbon whiskey is alcohol and water flavored with corn. These things they assert, and the great chemists do not enable us drinkers of those seductive liquids to deny it. On the contrary, chemical analysis, so far as it has gone, supports the teetotal view of the matter.

What does a glass of wine do to us when we have swallowed it?

We should naturally look to physicians for an answer to such a question; but the great lights of the profession — men of the rank of Astley Cooper, Brodie, Abernethy, Holmes — all assure the public, that no man of them knows, and no man has ever known, how medicinal substances work in the system, and why they produce the effects they do. Even of a substance so common as Peruvian bark, no one knows why and how it acts as a tonic; nor is there any certainty of its being a benefit to mankind. There is no science of medicine. The "Red Lane" of the children leads to a region which is still mysterious and unknown; for when the eye can explore its recesses, a change has occurred in it, which is also mysterious and unknown: it is dead. Quacks tell us, in every newspaper, that they can cure and prevent disease by pouring or dropping something down our throats, and we have heard this so often, that, when a man is sick, the first thing that occurs to him is to "take physic." But physicians who are honest, intelligent, and in an independent position, appear to be coming over to the opinion that this is generally a delusion. We see eminent physicians prescribing for the most malignant fevers little but open windows, plenty of blankets, Nightingale nursing, and beef tea. Many young physicians, too, have gladly availed themselves of the ingenuity of Hahnemann, and satisfy at once their consciences and their patients by prescribing doses of medicine that are next to no medicine at all. The higher we go among the doctors, the more sweeping and emphatic is the assurance we receive that the profession does not understand the operation of medicines in the living body, and does not really approve their employment.

If something more is known of the operation of

alcohol than of any other chemical fluid, — if there is any approach to certainty respecting it, — we owe it chiefly to the teetotalers, because it is they who have provoked contradiction, excited inquiry, and suggested experiment. They have not done much themselves in the way of investigation, but they started the topic, and have kept it alive. They have also published a few pages which throw light upon the points in dispute. After going over the ground pretty thoroughly, I can tell the reader in a few words the substance of what has been ascertained, and plausibly inferred, concerning the effects of wine, beer, and spirits upon the human constitution.

They cannot be *nourishment*, in the ordinary acceptation of that word, because the quantity of nutritive matter in them is so small. Liebig, no enemy of beer, says this: "We can prove, with mathematical certainty, that as much flour or meal as can lie on the point of a table-knife is more nutritious than nine quarts of the best Bavarian beer; that a man who is able daily to consume that amount of beer obtains from it, in a whole year, in the most favorable case, exactly the amount of nutritive constituents which is contained in a five-pound loaf of bread, or in three pounds of flesh." So of wine; when we have taken from a glass of wine the ingredients known to be innutritious, there is scarcely anything left but a grain or two of sugar. Pure alcohol, though a product of highly nutritive substances, is a mere poison, — an absolute poison, — the mortal foe of life in every one of its forms, animal and vegetable. If, therefore, these beverages do us good, it is not by supplying the body with nourishment.

Nor can they aid digestion by assisting to decompose food. When we have taken too much shad for breakfast, we find that a wineglass of whiskey instantly mitigates the horrors of indigestion, and enables us again to contemplate the future without dismay. But if we catch a curious fish or reptile, and want to keep him from decomposing, and bring him home as a contribution to the Museum of Professor Agassiz, we put him in a bottle of whiskey. Several experiments have been made with a view to ascertain whether mixing alcohol with the gastric juice increases or lessens its power to decompose food, and the results of all of them point to the conclusion that the alcohol retards the process of decomposition. A little alcohol retards it a little, and much alcohol retards it much. It has been proved by repeated experiment, that *any* portion of alcohol, however small, diminishes the power of the gastric juice to decompose. The digestive fluid has been mixed with wine, beer, whiskey, brandy, and alcohol diluted with water, and kept at the temperature of the living body, and the motions of the body imitated during the experiment; but, in every instance, the pure gastric juice was found to be the true and sole digester, and the alcohol a retarder of digestion. This fact, however, required little proof. We are all familiar with alcohol as a *preserver*, and scarcely need to be reminded, that, if alcohol assists digestion at all, it cannot be by assisting decomposition.

Nor is it a heat-producing fluid. On the contrary, it appears, in all cases, to diminish the efficiency of the heat-producing process. Most of us who live here in the North, and who are occasionally subjected to extreme cold for hours at a time, know this by personal experience; and all the Arctic voyagers attest it. Brandy is destruction when men have to face a temperature of sixty below zero; they want lamp-oil then, and the rich blubber of the whale and walrus. Dr. Rae, who made two or three pedestrian tours of the polar regions, and whose powers of endurance were put to as severe a test as man's ever were, is clear and emphatic upon this point. Brandy, he says, stimulates but for a few minutes, and greatly lessens a man's power to endure cold and fatigue. Occasionally we have in New York a cool breeze from the North which reduces the temperature below zero, — to the sore discomfort of omnibus-drivers and car-drivers, who have to face it on their way up town. On a certain Monday night, two or three winters ago, twenty-three drivers on one line were disabled by the cold, many of whom had to be lifted from the cars and carried in. It is a fact familiar to persons in this business, that men who drink freely are more likely to be benumbed and overcome by the cold than those who abstain. It seems strange to us, when we first hear it, that a meagre teetotaller should be safer on such a night than a bluff, red-faced imbiber of beer and whiskey, who takes something at each end of the line to keep himself warm. It nevertheless appears to be true. A traveller relates, that, when Russian troops are about to start upon a march in a very cold region, no grog is allowed to be served to them; and when the men are drawn up, ready to move, the corporals smell the breath of every man, and send back to quarters all who have been drinking. The reason is, that men who start under the influence of liquor are the first to succumb to the cold, and the likeliest to be frost-bitten. It is the uniform experience of the hunters and trappers in the northern provinces of North America, and of the Rocky Mountains, that alcohol diminishes their power to resist cold. A whole magazine could be filled with testimony on this point.

Still less is alcohol a strength-giver. Every man that ever trained for a supreme exertion of strength knows that Tom Sayers spoke the truth when he said: "I'm no teetotaller: but when I've any business to do, there's nothing like water and the dumb-bells." Richard Cobden, whose powers were subjected to a far severer trial than a pugilist ever dreamed of, whose labors by night and day, during the corn-law struggle, were excessive and continuous beyond those of any other member of the House of Commons, bears similar testimony: "The more work I have to do, the more I have resorted to the pump and the teapot." On this branch of the subject, *all* the testimony is against alcoholic drinks. Whenever the point has been tested, — and it has often been tested, — the truth has been confirmed, that he who would do his *very* best and most, whether in rowing, lifting, running, watching, mowing, climbing, fighting, speaking, or writing, must not admit into his system one drop of alcohol. Trainers used to allow their men a pint of beer per day, and severe trainers half a pint; but now the knowing ones have cut off even that moderate allowance, and brought their men down to cold water, and not too much of that, the soundest digesters requiring little liquid of any kind. Mr. Bigelow, by his happy publication lately of the correct version of Franklin's Autobiography, has called to mind the famous beer passage in that immortal work: "I drank only water; the other workmen, near fifty in number, were great guzzlers * of beer. On occasion I carried up and down stairs a large form of types in each hand, when others carried but one in both hands." I have a long list of references on this point; but, in these cricketing, boat-racing, prize-fighting days, the fact has become too familiar to require proof. The other morning, Horace Greeley, teetotaler, came to his office after an absence of several days, and found letters and arrears of work that would have been appalling to any man but him. He shut himself in at ten A. M., and wrote steadily, without leaving his room, till eleven, P. M., — thirteen hours. When he had finished, he had some little difficulty in getting down stairs, owing to the stiffness of his joints, caused by the long inaction; but he was as fresh and smiling the next morning as though he had done nothing extraordinary.

* We owe to Mr. Bigelow the restoration of this strong Franklinian word. The common editions have it "drinkers."

Are any of us drinkers of beer and wine capable of such a feat? Then, during the war, when he was writing his history, he performed every day, for two years, two days' work, — one from nine to four, on his book; the other from seven to eleven, upon the Tribune; and, in addition, he did more than would tire an ordinary man in the way of correspondence and public speaking. I may also remind the reader, that the clergyman who, of all others in the United States, expends most vitality, both with tongue and pen, and who does his work with least fatigue and most gayety of heart, is another of Franklin's "water Americans."

If, then, wine does not nourish us, does not assist the decomposition of food, does not warm, does not strengthen, what does it do?

We all know that, when we drink alcoholic liquor, it affects the brain immediately. Most of us are aware, too, that it affects the brain injuriously, lessening at once its power to discern and discriminate. If I, at this ten, A. M., full of interest in this subject, and eager to get my view of it upon paper, were to drink a glass of the best port, Madeira, or sherry, or even a glass of lager-bier, I should lose the power to continue in three minutes; or, if I persisted in going on, I should be pretty sure to utter paradox and spurts of extravagance, which would not bear the cold review of to-morrow morning. Any one can try this experiment. Take two glasses of wine, and then immediately apply yourself to the hardest task your mind ever has to perform, and you will find you cannot do it. Let any student, just before he sits down to his mathematics, drink a pint of the purest beer, and he will be painfully conscious of loss of power. Or, let any salesman, before beginning with a difficult but important customer, perform the idiotic action of "taking a drink," and he will soon discover that his ascendency over his customer is impaired. In some way this alcohol, of which we are so fond, gets to the brain and injures it. We are conscious of this, and we can observe it. It is among the wine-drinking classes of our fellow-beings, that absurd, incomplete, and reactionary ideas prevail. The receptive, the curious, the candid, the trustworthy brains, — those that do not take things for granted, and yet are ever open to conviction, — such heads are to be found on the shoulders of men who drink little or none of these seductive fluids. How we all wondered that England should *think* so erroneously, and adhere to its errors so obstinately, during our late war! Mr. Gladstone has in part explained the mystery. The adults of England, he said, in his famous wine speech, drink, on an average, three hundred quarts of beer each per annum! Now, it is physically impossible for a human brain, muddled every day with a quart of beer, to correctly hold correct opinions, or appropriate pure knowledge. Compare the conversation of a group of Vermont farmers, gathered on the stoop of a country store on a rainy afternoon, with that which you may hear in the farmers' room of a market-town inn in England! The advantage is not wholly with the Vermonters; by no means, for there is much in human nature besides the brain and the things of the brain. But in this one particular — in the topics of conversation, in the interest manifested in large and important subjects — the water-drinking Vermonters are to the beer-drinking Englishmen what Franklin was to the London printers. It is beyond the capacity of a well-beered brain even to read the pamphlet on Liberty and Necessity which Franklin wrote in those times.

The few experiments which have been made, with a view to trace the course of alcohol in the living system, all confirm what all drinkers feel, that it is to the brain alcohol hurries when it has passed the lips. Some innocent dogs have suffered and died in this investigation. Dr. Percy, a British physician, records, that he injected two ounces and a half of alcohol into the stomach of a dog, which caused its almost instant death. The dog dropped very much as he would if he had been struck upon the head with a club. The experimenter, without a moment's unnecessary delay, removed the animal's brain, subjected it to distillation, and extracted from it a surprising quantity of alcohol, — a larger proportion than he could distil from the blood or liver. The alcohol seemed to have rushed to the brain: it *was* a blow upon the head which killed the dog. Dr. Percy introduced into the stomachs of other dogs smaller quantities of alcohol, not sufficient to cause death; but upon killing the dogs, and subjecting the brain, the blood, the bile, the liver, and other portions of the body, to distillation, he invariably found more alcohol in the brain than in the same weight of other organs. He injected alcohol into the blood of dogs, which caused death; but the deadly effect was produced, not upon the substance of the blood, but upon the brain. His experiments go far toward explaining why the drinking of alcoholic liquors does not sensibly retard digestion. It seems that, when we take wine at dinner, the alcohol does not remain in the stomach, but is immediately absorbed into the blood, and swiftly conveyed to the brain and other organs. If one of those "four-bottle men" of the last generation had fallen down dead, after boozing till past midnight, and he had been treated as Dr. Percy treated the dogs, his brain, his liver, and all the other centres of power, would have yielded alcohol in abundance; his blood would have smelt of it; his flesh would have contained it; but there would have been very little in the stomach. Those men were able to drink four, six, and seven bottles of wine at a sitting, because the sitting lasted four, six, and seven hours, which gave time for the alcohol to be distributed over the system. But instances have occurred of laboring men who have kept themselves steadily drunk for forty-eight hours, and then died. The bodies of two such were dissected some years ago in England, and the food which they had eaten at the beginning of the debauch was undigested. It had been preserved in alcohol as we preserve snakes.

Once, and only once, in the lifetime of man, an intelligent human eye has been able to look into the living stomach, and watch the process of digestion. In 1822, at the United States military post of Michilimackinac, Alexis St. Martin, a Canadian of French extraction, received accidentally a heavy charge of duck-shot in his side, while he was standing one yard from the muzzle of the gun. The wound was frightful. One of the lungs protruded, and from an enormous aperture in the stomach the food recently eaten was oozing. Dr. William Beaumont, U. S. A., the surgeon of the post, was notified, and dressed the wound. In exactly one year from that day the young man was well enough to get out of doors, and walk about the fort; and he continued to improve in health and strength, until he was as strong and hardy as most of his race. He married, became the father of a large family, and performed for many years the laborious duties appertaining to an officer's servant at a frontier post. But the aperture into the stomach never closed, and the patient would not submit to the painful operation by which such wounds are sometimes closed artificially. He wore a compress arranged by the doctor, without which his dinner was not safe after he had eaten it.

By a most blessed chance it happened that this Dr. William Beaumont, stationed there on the outskirts of creation, was an intelligent, inquisitive human being, who perceived all the value of the opportunity afforded him by this unique event. He set about improving that opportunity. He took the young man into his service, and, at intervals, for eight years, he experimented upon him. He alone among the sons of men has seen liquid flowing into the stomach of a living person while yet the vessel was at the drinker's lips. Through the aperture (which remained two and a half inches in circumference) he could watch the entire operation of digestion, and he did so hundreds of times. If the man's stomach ached, he could look into it and see what was the matter; and, having found out, he would drop a rectifying pill into the aperture. He ascertained the time it takes to digest each of the articles of food commonly eaten, and the effects of all the usual errors in eating and drinking. In 1833, he published a thin volume, at Plattsburg on Lake Champlain, in which the results of thousands of experiments and observations were only too briefly stated. He appears not to have heard of teetotalism, and hence all that he says upon the effects of alcoholic liquors is free from the suspicion which the arrogance and extravagance of some teetotalers have thrown over much that has been published on this subject. With a mind unbiassed, Dr. Beaumont, peering into the stomach of this stout Canadian, notices that a glass of brandy causes the coats of that organ to assume the same inflamed appearance as when he had been very angry, or much frightened, or had overeaten, or had had the flow of perspiration suddenly checked. In other words, brandy played the part of a *foe* in his system, not that of a friend; it produced effects which were morbid, not healthy. Nor did it make any material difference whether St. Martin drank brandy, whiskey, wine, cider, or beer, except so far as one was stronger than the other.

"Simple water," says Dr. Beaumont, "is perhaps the only fluid that is called for by the wants of the economy. The artificial drinks are probably *all* more or less injurious; some more so than others, but none can claim exemption from the general charge. Even tea and coffee, the common beverages of all classes of people, have a tendency to debilitate the digestive organs. . . . . The whole class of alcoholic liquors may be considered as narcotics, producing very little difference in their ultimate effects upon the system."

He ascertained too (not guessed, or inferred, but *ascertained*, watch in hand) that such things as mustard, horse-radish, and pepper retard digestion. At the close of his invaluable work Dr. Beaumont appends a long list of " Inferences," among which are the following: " That solid food of a certain texture is easier of digestion than fluid ; that stimulating condiments are injurious to the healthy system ; that the use of ardent spirits *always* produces disease of the stomach if persisted in ; that water, ardent spirits, and most other fluids, are not affected by the gastric juice, but pass from the stomach soon after they have been received." One thing appears to have much surprised Dr. Beaumont, and that was, the degree to which St. Martin's system could be disordered without his being much inconvenienced by it. After drinking hard every day for eight or ten days, the stomach would show alarming appearances of disease; and yet the man would only feel a slight headache, and a general dulness and languor.

If there is no comfort for drinkers in Dr. Beaumont's precious little volume, it must be also confessed, that neither the dissecting-knife nor the microscope afford us the least countenance. All that has yet been ascertained of the effects of alcohol by the dissection of the body favors the extreme position of the extreme teetotalers. A brain alcoholized the microscope proves to be a brain diseased. Blood which has absorbed alcohol is unhealthy blood, — the microscope shows it. The liver, the heart, and other organs, which have been accustomed to absorb alcohol, all give testimony under the microscope which produces discomfort in the mind of one who likes a glass of wine, and hopes to be able to continue the enjoyment of it. The dissecting-knife and the microscope so far have nothing to say for us, — nothing at all: they are dead against us.

Of all the experiments which have yet been undertaken with a view to trace the course of alcohol through the human system, the most important were those made in Paris a few years ago by Professors Lallemand, Perrin, and Duroy, distinguished physicians and chemists. Frenchmen have a way of co-operating with one another, both in the investigation of scientific questions and in the production of literature, which is creditable to their civilization and beneficial to the world. The experiments conducted by these gentlemen produced the remarkable effect of causing the editor of a leading periodical to confess to the public that he was not infallible. In 1855 the Westminster Review contained an article by Mr. Lewes, in which the teetotal side of these questions was effectively ridiculed; but, in 1861, the same periodical reviewed the work of the French professors just named, and honored itself by appending a note in which it said: "Since the date of our former article, scientific research has brought to light important facts which necessarily modify the opinions we then expressed concerning the *rôle* of alcohol in the animal body." Those facts were revealed or indicated in the experiments of Messrs. Lallemand, Perrin, and Duroy.

Ether and chloroform, — their mode of operation; why and how they render the living body insensible to pain under the surgeon's knife; what becomes of them after they have performed that office, — these were the points which engaged their attention, and in the investigation of which they spent several years. They were rewarded, at length, with the success due to patience and ingenuity. By the aid of ingenious apparatus, after experiments almost numberless, they felt themselves in a position to demonstrate, that, when ether is inhaled, it is immediately absorbed by the blood, and by the blood is conveyed to the brain. If a surgeon were to commit such a breach of professional etiquette as to cut off a patient's head at the moment of complete insensibility, he would be able to distil from the brain a great quantity of ether. But it is not usual to take that liberty except with dogs. The inhalation, therefore, proceeds until the surgical operation is finished, when the handkerchief is withdrawn from the patient's face, and he is left to regain his senses. What happens then? What becomes of the ether? These learned Frenchmen discovered that most of it goes out of the body by the road it came in at, — the lungs. It was breathed in; it is breathed out. The rest escapes by other channels of egress; it all escapes, and it escapes unchanged! That is the point: it escapes without having *left* anything in the system. All that can be said of it is, that it entered the body, created morbid conditions in the body, and then left the body. It cost these patient men years to arrive at this result; but any one who has ever had charge of a patient that has been rendered insensible by ether will find little difficulty in believing it.

Having reached this demonstration, the experimenters naturally thought of applying the same method and similar apparatus to the investigation of the effects of alcohol, which is the fluid nearest resembling ether and chloroform. Dogs and men suffered in the cause. In the moisture exhaled from the pores of a drunken dog's skin, these cunning Frenchmen detected the alcohol which had made him drunk. They proved it to exist in the breath of a man, at six o'clock in the evening, who had drunk a bottle of claret for breakfast at half past ten in the morning. They also proved that, at midnight, the alcohol of that bottle of wine was still availing itself of other avenues of escape. They proved that when alcohol is taken into the system in any of its dilutions, — wine, cider, spirits, or beer, — the whole animal economy speedily busies itself with its expulsion, and continues to do so until it has expelled it. The lungs exhale it; the pores of the skin let out a little of it; the kidneys do their part; and by whatever other road an enemy can escape it seeks the outer air. Like ether, alcohol enters the body, makes a disturbance there, and goes out of the body, leaving it no richer than it found it. It is a guest that departs, after giving a great deal of trouble, without paying his bill or "remembering" the servants. Now, to make the demonstration complete, it would be necessary to take some unfortunate man or dog, give him a certain quantity of alcohol, — say one ounce, — and afterwards distil from his breath, perspiration, &c., the whole quantity that he had swallowed. This has not been done; it never will be done; it is obviously impossible. Enough has been done to justify these conscientious and indefatigable inquirers in announcing, as a thing susceptible of all but demonstration, that alcohol contributes to the human system nothing whatever, but leaves it undigested and wholly unchanged. They are fully persuaded (and so will you be, reader, if you read their book) that, if you take into your system an ounce of alcohol, the whole ounce leaves the system within forty-eight hours, just as good alcohol as it went in.

There is a boy in Pickwick who swallowed a farthing. "Out with it," said the father; and it is to be presumed — though Mr. Weller does not mention the fact — that the boy complied with a request so reasonable. Just as much nutrition as that small copper coin left in the system of that boy, plus a small lump of sugar, did the claret which we drank yesterday deposit in ours; so, at least, we must infer from the experiments of Messrs. Lallemand, Perrin, and Duroy.

To evidence of this purely scientific nature might be added, if space could be afforded, a long list of persons who, having indulged in wine for many years, have found benefit from discontinuing the use of it. Most of us have known such instances. I have known several, and I can most truly say, that I have never known an individual in tolerable health who discontinued the use of any stimulant whatever without benefit. We all remember Sydney Smith's strong sentences on this point, scattered through the volume which contains the correspondence of that delicious humorist and wit. "I like London better than ever I liked it before," he writes in the prime of his prime (forty-three years old) to Lady Holland, "and simply, I believe, from water-drinking. Without this, London is stupefaction and inflammation." So has New York become. Again, in 1828, when he was fifty-seven, to the same lady: "I not only was never better, but never half so well; indeed, I find I have been very ill all my life without knowing it. Let me state some of the goods arising from abstaining from all fermented liquors. First, sweet sleep; having never known what sweet sleep was, I sleep like a baby or a plough-boy. If I wake, no needless terrors, no black visions of life, but pleasing hopes and pleasing recollections: Holland House past and to come! If I dream, it is not of lions and tigers, but of Easter dues and tithes. Secondly, I can take longer walks and make greater exertions without fatigue. My understanding is improved, and I comprehend political economy. I see better without wine and spectacles than when I used both. Only one evil ensues from it; I am in such extravagant spirits that I must lose blood, or look out for some one who will boré or depress me. Pray leave off wine: the stomach is quite at rest; no heartburn, no pain, no distention."

I have also a short catalogue of persons who, having long lived innocent of these agreeable drinks, began at length to use them. Dr. Franklin's case is striking. That "water American," as he was styled by the London printers, whose ceaseless guzzling of beer he ridiculed in his twentieth year, drank wine in his sixtieth with the freedom usual at that period among persons of good estate. "At parting," he writes in 1768, when he was sixty-two, "after we had drank a bottle and a half of claret each, Lord Clare hugged and kissed me, protesting he never in his life met with a man he was so much in love with." The consequence of this departure from the customs of his earlier life was ten years of occasional acute torture from the stone and gravel. Perhaps, if Franklin had remained a "water American," he would have annexed Canada to the United States at the peace of 1782.

An agonizing attack of stone laid him on his back for three months, just as the negotiation was becoming interesting; and by the time he was well again the threads were gone out of his hands into those of the worst diplomatists that ever threw a golden chance away.

What are we to conclude from all this? Are we to knock the heads out of all our wine-casks, join the temperance society, and denounce all men who do not follow our example? Taking together all that science and observation teach and indicate, we have one certainty: That, to a person in good health and of good life, alcoholic liquors are not necessary, but are always in some degree hurtful. This truth becomes so clear, after a few weeks' investigation, that I advise every person who means to keep on drinking such liquors not to look into the facts; for if he does, he will never again be able to lift a glass of wine to his lips, nor contemplate a foaming tankard, nor mix his evening toddy, nor hear the pop and melodious gurgle of champagne, with that fine complacency which irradiates his countenance now, and renders it so pleasing a study to those who sit on the other side of the table. No; never again! Even the flavor of those fluids will lose something of their charm. The conviction will obtrude itself upon his mind at most inopportune moments, that this drinking of wine, beer, and whiskey, to which we are so much addicted, is an enormous delusion. If the teetotalers would induce some rational being — say that public benefactor, Dr.

Willard **Parker of New York** — to collect into one small volume the substance of all the investigations alluded to in this article, — the substance of Dr. Beaumont's precious little book, the substance of the French professors' work, and the others, — adding no comment except such **as** might be necessary to elucidate the investigators' meaning, it could not but carry conviction to every candid and intelligent reader that spirituous drinks are to the healthy system an injury necessarily, and in all cases.

The Coming Man, then, so long as he enjoys good health, — which he usually will from infancy to hoary age, — will *not* drink wine, nor, of course, any of the coarser alcoholic dilutions. To that unclouded and fearless intelligence, science will be the supreme law; it will be to him more than the Koran is to a Mohammedan, and more than the Infallible Church is to a Roman Catholic. Science, or, in other words, the **law of God as** revealed in nature, life, and history, and as ascertained by experiment, observation, and thought, — this will be the teacher and guide of the Coming Man.

A single certainty in a matter of so much importance is not to be despised. I can now say to young fellows who order a bottle of wine, and flatter themselves that, in **so** doing, they approve themselves "jolly dogs": No, **my** lads, it is **because** you are dull dogs **that** you want **the wine. You** are forced to borrow **excitement because you have** squandered your natural **gayety.** The ordering of the wine is a confession of insolvency. When we feel it necessary to "take something" at certain times during the day, we are in a condition similar to that of a merchant who every day, about the anxious hour of half past two, has to run around among his neighbors borrowing credit. It is something disgraceful or suspicious. Nature does not supply enough of inward force. We are in arrears. Our condition is absurd; and, if we ought not to be alarmed, we ought at least to be ashamed. Nor does the borrowed credit increase our store; it leaves nothing behind to enrich *us*, but takes something from our already insufficient stock; and the more pressing our need the more it costs us to borrow.

But the Coming Man, blooming, robust, alert, and light-hearted as he will be, may not be always well. If, as he springs up a mountain-side, his foot slips, the law of gravitation will respect nature's darling too much to keep him from tumbling down the precipice; and, as he wanders in strange regions, an unperceived malaria may poison his pure and vivid blood. Some generous errors, too, he may commit (although it is not probable), and expend a portion of his own life in warding off evil from the lives of others. Fever may blaze even in his clear eyes; poison may rack his magnificent frame, and a long convalescence may severely try his admirable patience. Will the Coming Man drink wine when he is sick? The question is not easily answered.

One valuable witness on this branch of the inquiry is the late Theodore Parker. A year or two before his lamented death, when he was already struggling with the disease that terminated his existence, he wrote for his friend, Dr. Bowditch, "the consumptive history" of his family from 1634, when his stalwart English ancestor settled in New England. The son of that ancestor built a house, in 1664, upon the slope of a hill which terminated in "a great fresh meadow of spongy peat," which was "always wet all the year through," and from which "fogs could be seen gathering towards night of a clear day."* In the third generation of the occupants of this house consumption was developed, and carried off eight children out of eleven, all between the ages of sixteen and nineteen. From that time consumption was the bane of the race, and spared not the offspring of parents who had removed from the family seat into localities free from malaria. One of the daughters of the house, who married a man of giant stature and great strength, became the mother of four sons. Three of these sons, though settled in a healthy place and in an innoxious business, died of consumption between twenty and twenty-five. But the fourth son became intemperate, — drank great quantities of New England rum. He did *not* die of the disease, but was fifty-five years of age when the account was written, and then exhibited no consumptive tendency! To this fact Mr. Parker added others : —

"1. I know a consumptive family living in a situa-

* Life and Correspondence of Theodore Parker. By John Weiss. Vol. II. p. 513.

tion like that I have mentioned for, perhaps, the same length of time, who had four sons. Two of them were often drunk, and always intemperate,—one of them as long as I can remember; both consumptive in early life, but now both hearty men from sixty to seventy. The two others were temperate, one drinking moderately, the other but occasionally. They both died of consumption, the eldest not over forty-five.

"2. Another consumptive family in such a situation as has been already described had many sons and several daughters. The daughters were all temperate, married, settled elsewhere, had children, died of consumption, bequeathing it also to their posterity. But five of the sons, whom I knew, were drunkards, — some, of the extremest description; they all had the consumptive build, and in early life showed signs of the disease, but none of them died of it; some of them are still burning in rum. There was one brother temperate, a farmer, living in the healthiest situation. But I was told he died some years ago of consumption."

To these facts must be added one more woful than a thousand such,—that Theodore Parker himself, one of the most valuable lives upon the Western Continent, died of consumption in his fiftieth year. The inference which Mr. Parker drew from the family histories given was the following: "Intemperate habits (where the man drinks a pure, though coarse and fiery, liquor, like New England rum) tend to check the consumptive tendency, though the drunkard, who himself escapes the consequences, may transmit the fatal seed to his children."

There is not much comfort in this for topers; but the facts are interesting, and have their value. A similar instance is related by Mr. Charles Knight; although in this case the poisoned air was more deadly, and more swift to destroy. Mr. Knight speaks, in his Popular History of England, of the "careless and avaricious employers" of London, among whom, he says, the master-tailors were the most notorious. Some of them would "huddle sixty or eighty workmen close together, nearly knee to knee, in a room fifty feet long by twenty feet broad, lighted from above, where the temperature in summer was thirty degrees higher than the temperature outside. Young men from the country fainted when they were first confined in such a life-destroying prison; the maturer ones *sustained themselves by gin*, till they perished of consumption, or typhus, or delirium tremens."

To a long list of such facts as these could be added instances in which the deadly agent was other than poisoned air,— excessive exertion, very bad food, gluttony, deprivation. During the war I knew of a party of cavalry who, for three days and three nights, were not out of the saddle fifteen minutes at a time. The men consumed two quarts of whiskey each, and all of them came in alive. It is a custom in England to extract the last possible five miles from a tired horse, when those miles *must* be had from him, by forcing down his most unwilling throat a quart of beer. It is known, too, that life can be sustained for many years in considerable vigor, upon a remarkably short allowance of food, provided the victim keeps his system well saturated with alcohol. Travellers across the plains to California tell us that, soon after getting past St. Louis, they strike a region where the principal articles of diet are saleratus and grease, to which a little flour and pork are added; upon which, they say, human life cannot be sustained unless the natural waste of the system is retarded by "preserving" the tissues in whiskey. Mr. Greeley, however, got through alive without resorting to this expedient, but he confesses in one of his letters that he suffered pangs and horrors of indigestion.

All such facts as these — and they could be collected in great numbers — indicate the real office of alcohol in our modern life: *It enables us to violate the laws of nature without immediate suffering and speedy destruction.* This appears to be its chief office, in conjunction with its ally, tobacco. Those tailors would have soon died or escaped but for the gin; and those horsemen would have given up and perished but for the whiskey. Nature commanded those soldiers to rest, but they were enabled, for the moment, to disobey her. Doubtless Nature was even with them afterwards; but, for the time, they *could* defy their mother great and wise. Alcohol supported them in doing wrong. Alcohol and tobacco support half the modern world in doing wrong. That is their part — their *rôle*, as the French investigators term it — in the present life of the human race.

Dr. Great Practice would naturally go to bed at ten o'clock, when he comes in from his evening visits. It is his cigar that keeps him up till half past twelve, writing those treatises which make him famous, and shorten his life. Lawyer Heavy Fee takes home his papers, pores over them till past one, and then depends upon whiskey to quiet his brain and put him to sleep. Young Bohemian gets away from the office of the morning paper which enjoys the benefit of his fine talents at three o'clock. It is two mugs of lager-bier which enable him to endure the immediate consequences of eating a supper before going home. This is mad work, my masters; it is respectable suicide, nothing better.

There is a paragraph now making the grand tour of the newspapers, which informs the public that there was a dinner given the other evening in New York consisting of twelve courses, and keeping the guests five hours at the table. For five hours, men and women sat consuming food, occupying half an hour at each viand. What could sustain human nature in such an amazing effort? What could enable them to look into one another's faces without blushing scarlet at the infamy of such a waste of time, food, and digestive force? What concealed from them the iniquity and deep vulgarity of what they were doing? The explanation of this mystery is given in the paragraph that records the crime: "There was a different kind of wine for each course."

Even an ordinary dinner-party, — what mortal could eat it through, or sit it out, without a constant sipping of wine to keep his brain muddled, and lash his stomach to unnatural exertion. The joke of it is, that we all know and confess to one another how absurd such banquets are, and yet few have the courage and humanity to feed their friends in a way which they can enjoy, and feel the better for the next morning.

When I saw Mr. Dickens eating and drinking his way through the elegantly bound book which Mr. Delmonico substituted for the usual bill of fare at the dinner given by the Press last April to the great artist, — a task of three hours' duration, — when, I say, I saw Mr. Dickens thus engaged, I wondered which banquet was the furthest from being the right thing, — the one to which he was then vainly trying to do justice, or the one of which Martin Chuzzlewit partook, on the day he landed in New York, at Mrs. Pawkins's boarding-house. The poultry, on the latter occasion, "disappeared as if every bird had had the use of its wings, and had flown in desperation down a human throat. The oysters, stewed and pickled, leaped from their capacious reservoirs, and slid by scores into the mouths of the assembly. The sharpest pickles vanished, whole cucumbers at once, like sugar-plums, and no man winked his eye. Great heaps of indigestible matter melted away as ice before the sun. It was a solemn and an awful thing to see." Of course, the company adjourned from the dining-room to "the bar-room in the next block," where they imbibed strong drink enough to keep their dinner from prostrating them.

The Delmonico banquet was a very different affair. Our public dinners are all arranged on the English system; for we have not yet taken up with the fine, sweeping principle, that whatever is right for England is wrong for America. Hence, not a lady was present! Within a day's journey of New York there are about thirty ladies who write regularly for the periodical press, besides as many more, perhaps, who contribute to it occasionally. Many editors, too, derive constant and important assistance, in the exercise of their profession, from their wives and daughters, who read books for them, suggest topics, correct errors, and keep busy editors in mind of the great truth that more than one half the human race is female. Mrs. Kemble, who had a treble claim to a seat at that table, was not many miles distant. Why were none of these gifted ladies present to grace and enliven the scene? The true answer is: *Wine and smoke!* Not *our* wine and smoke, but those of our British ancestors who invented public dinners. The hospitable young gentlemen who had the affair in charge would have been delighted, no doubt, to depart from the established system, but hardly liked to risk so tremendous an innovation on an occasion of so much interest. If it had been put to the vote (by ballot), when the company had assembled, Shall we have ladies or not? all the hard drinkers, all the old smokers, would have furtively written "not" upon their ballots. Those who drink little wine, and do not depend upon that little; those who do not smoke or can easily dispense with smoke,—would have voted for the ladies; and the ladies would have carried the day by the majority which is so hard to get,—two thirds.

It was a wise man who discovered that a small quantity of excellent soup is a good thing to begin a dinner with. He deserves well of his species. The soup allays the hungry savage within us, and restores us to civilization and to one another. Nor is he to be reckoned a traitor to his kind who first proclaimed that a little very nice and dainty fish, hot and crisp from the fire, is a pleasing introduction to more substantial viands. Six oysters upon their native shell, fresh from their ocean home, and freshly opened, small in size, intense in flavor, cool, but not too cold, radiating from a central quarter of a lemon,—this, too, was a fine conception, worthy of the age in which we live. But in what language can we characterize aright the abandoned man who first presumed to tempt Christians to begin a repast by partaking of *all* three of these,— oysters, soup, *and* fish? The object is defeated. The true purpose of these introductory trifles is to appease the appetite in a slight degree, so as to enable us to take sustenance with composure and dignity, and dispose the company to conversation. When a properly constituted person has eaten six oysters, a plate of soup, and the usual portion of fish, with the proper quantity of potatoes and bread, he has taken as much sustenance as nature requires. All the rest of the banquet is excess; and being excess, it is also mistake; it is a diminution of the sum-total of pleasure which the repast was capable of affording. But when Mr. Delmonico had brought us successfully so far on our way through his book; when we had consumed our oysters, our cream of asparagus in the Dumas style, our kettle-drums in the manner of Charles Dickens, and our trout cooked so as to do honor to Queen Victoria, we had only picked up a few pebbles on the shore of the banquet, while the great ocean of food still stretched out before us illimitable. The fillet of beef after the manner of Lucullus, the stuffed lamb in the style of Sir Walter Scott, the cutlets à la Fenimore Cooper, the historic pâtés, the sighs of Mantalini, and a dozen other efforts of Mr. Delmonico's genius, remained to be attempted.

No man would willingly eat or sit through such a dinner without plenty of wine, which here plays its natural part,—supporting us in doing wrong. It is the wine which enables people to keep on eating for three hours, and to cram themselves with highly concentrated food, without rolling on the floor in agony. It is the wine which puts it within our power to consume, in digesting one dinner, the force that would suffice for the digestion of three.

On that occasion Mr. Dickens was invited to visit us every twenty-five years "for the rest of his life," to see how we are getting on. The Coming Man may be a guest at the **farewell** banquet which the Press will give to the venerable author in 1893. That banquet will consist of three courses; and, instead of seven kinds of wine and various brands of cigars, there will be at every table its due proportion of ladies, the ornaments of their own sex, the instructors of ours, the boast and glory of the future Press of America.

Wine, ale, and liquors, administered strictly as medicine, — what of them? Doctors differ on the subject, and known facts point to different conclusions. Distinguished physicians in England are of the opinion that Prince Albert would be alive at this moment if *no* wine had been given him during his last sickness; but there were formerly those who thought that the Princess Charlotte would have been saved, if, at the crisis of her malady, she could have *had* the glass of port wine which she craved and asked for. The biographers of William Pitt — Lord Macaulay among them — tell us, that at fourteen that precocious youth was tormented by inherited gout, and that the doctors prescribed a hair of the same dog which had bitten his ancestor from whom the gout was derived. The boy, we are told, used to consume two bottles of port a day; and, after keeping up this regimen for several months, he recovered his health, and retained it until, at the age of forty-seven, the news of Ulm and Austerlitz struck him mortal blows. Professor James Miller, of the University of Edinburgh, a decided teetotaler, declares *for* wine in bad cases of fever; but

Dr. R. T. Trall, another teetotaler, says that during the last twenty years he has treated hundreds of cases of fevers on the cold-water system, and "not yet lost the first one"; although, during the first ten years of his practice, when he gave wine and other stimulants, he lost "about the usual proportion of cases." The truth appears to be that, in a few instances of intermittent disease, a small quantity of wine may sometimes enable a patient who is at the low tide of vitality to anticipate the turn of the tide, and borrow at four o'clock enough of five o'clock strength to enable him to reach five o'clock. With regard to this daily drinking of wine and whiskey, by ladies and others, for mere debility, it is a delusion. In such cases wine is, in the most literal sense of the word, a mocker. It seems to nourish, but does not; it seems to warm, but does not; it seems to strengthen, but does not. It is an arrant cheat, and perpetuates the evils it is supposed to alleviate.

The Coming Man, as before remarked, will not drink wine when he is well. It will be also an article of his religion not to commit any of those sins against his body the consequences of which can be postponed by drinking wine. He will hold his body in veneration. He will feel all the turpitude and shame of violating it. He will not acquire the greatest intellectual good by the smallest bodily loss. He will know that mental acquisitions gained at the expense of physical power or prowess are not culture, but effeminacy. He will honor a rosy and stalwart ignoramus, who is also an honest man, faithfully standing at his post; but he will start back with affright and indignation at the spectacle of a pallid philosopher. The Coming Man, I am firmly persuaded, will not drink wine, nor any other stimulating fluid. If by chance he should be sick, he will place himself in the hands of the Coming Doctor, and take whatever is prescribed. The impression is strong upon my mind, after reading almost all there is in print on the subject, and conversing with many physicians, that the Coming Doctor will give his patients alcoholic mixtures about as often as he will give them laudanum, and in doses of about the same magnitude, reckoned by drops.

We drinkers have been in the habit, for many years, of playing off the wine countries against the teetotalers; but even this argument fails us when we question the men who really know the wine countries. Alcohol appears to be as pernicious to man in Italy, France, and Southern Germany, where little is taken except in the form of wine, as it is in Sweden, Scotland, Russia, England, and the United States, where more fiery and powerful dilutions are usual. Fenimore Cooper wrote: "I came to Europe under the impression that there was more drunkenness among us than in any other country, — England, perhaps, excepted. A residence of six months in Paris changed my views entirely; I have taken unbelievers with me into the streets, and have never failed to convince them of their mistake in the course of an hour. . . . . On one occasion a party of four went out with this object; we passed thirteen drunken men within a walk of an hour, — many of them were so far gone as to be totally unable to walk. . . . . In passing between Paris and London, I have been more struck by drunkenness in the streets of the former than in those of the latter." Horatio Greenough gives similar testimony respecting Italy: "Many of the more thinking and prudent Italians abstain from the use of wine; several of the most eminent of the medical men are notoriously opposed to its use, and declare it a poison. One fifth, and sometimes one fourth, of the earnings of the laborers are expended in wine."

I have been surprised at the quantity, the emphasis, and the uniformity of the testimony on this point. Close observers of the famous beer countries, such as Saxony and Bavaria, where the beer is pure and excellent, speak of this delicious liquid as the chief enemy of the nobler faculties and tastes of human nature. The surplus wealth, the surplus time, the surplus force of those nations, are chiefly expended in fuddling the brain with beer. Now, no reader needs to be informed that the progress of man, of nations, and of men depends upon the use they make of their little surplus. It is not a small matter, but a great and weighty consideration, — the cost of these drinks in mere money. We drinkers must make out a very clear case in order to justify such a country as France in producing a *billion and a half of dollars'* worth of wine and brandy per annum.

The teetotalers, then, are right in their leading positions, and yet they stand aghast, wondering at their failure to convince mankind. Mr. E. G. Delavan writes from Paris within these few weeks: " When I was here thirty years since, Louis Philippe told me that wine was the curse of France ; that he wished every grape-vine was destroyed, except for the production of food ; that total abstinence was the only true temperance ; but he did not believe there were fifteen persons in Paris who understood it as it was understood by his family and myself ; but he hoped from the labors in America, in time, an influence would flow back upon France that would be beneficial. I am here again after the lapse of so many years, and in place of witnessing any abatement of the evil, I think it is on the increase, especially in the use of distilled spirits."

The teetotalers have underrated the difficulty of the task they have undertaken, and misconceived its nature. It is not the great toe that most requires treatment when a man has the gout, although it is the great toe that makes him roar. When we look about us, and consider the present physical life of man, we are obliged to conclude that the whole head is sick and the whole heart is faint. Drinking is but a symptom which reveals the malady. Perhaps, if we were all to stop our guzzling suddenly, *without* discontinuing our other bad habits, we should rather lose by it than gain. Alcohol supports us in doing wrong! It prevents our immediate destruction. The thing for us to do is, to strike at the causes of drinking, to cease the bad breathing, the bad eating, the bad reading, the bad feeling and bad thinking, which, in a sense, necessitate bad drinking. For some of the teetotal organizations might be substituted Physical Welfare Societies.

The Human Race is now on trial for its life! One hundred and three years ago last April, James Watt, a poor Scotch mechanic, while taking his walk on Sunday afternoon on Glasgow Green, conceived the idea which has made steam man's submissive and untiring slave. Steam enables the fifteen millions of adults in Great Britain and Ireland to produce more commodities than the whole population of the earth could produce without its assistance. Steam, plus the virgin soil of two new continents, has placed the means of self-destruction within the reach of hundreds of millions of human beings whose ancestors were almost as safe in their ignorance and poverty as the beasts they attended. At the same time, the steam-engine is an infuriate propagator; and myriad creatures of its producing — creatures of eager desires, thin brains, excessive vanity, and small self-control — seem formed to bend the neck to the destructive tyranny of fashion, and yield helplessly to the more destructive tyranny of habit. The steam-engine gives them a great variety of the means of self-extirpation, — air-tight houses, labor-saving machines, luxurious food, stimulating drinks, highly wrought novels, and many others. Let all women for the next century but wear such restraining clothes as are now usual, and it is doubtful if the race could ever recover from the effects; it is doubtful if there could ever again be a full-orbed, bouncing baby. Wherever we look, we see the human race dwindling. The English aristocracy used to be thought an exception, but Miss Nightingale says not. She tells us that the great houses of England, like the small houses of America, contain great-grandmothers possessing constitutions without a flaw, grandmothers but slightly impaired, mothers who are often ailing and never strong, daughters who are miserable and hopeless invalids. And the steam-engine has placed efficient means of self-destruction within reach of the kitchen, the stable, the farm, and the shop ; and those means of self-destruction are all but universally used.

Perhaps man has nearly run his course in this world, and is about to disappear, like the mammoth, and give place to some nobler kind of creature who will manage the estate better than the present occupant. Certainly we cannot boast of having done very well with it, nor could we complain if we should receive notice to leave. Perhaps James Watt came into the world to extinguish his species. If so, it is well. Let us go on eating, drinking, smoking, over-working, idling, men killing themselves to buy clothes for their wives, wives killing themselves by wearing them, children petted and candied into imbecility and diphtheria. In that case, of course, there will be no Coming Man, and we need not take the trouble to inquire what he will do.

But probably the instinct of self-preservation will assert itself in time, and an antidote to the steam-engine will be **found before it has** impaired the whole race beyond recovery. To have discovered the truth **with** regard **to** the effects of alcohol upon the system was **of** itself **no** slight triumph of the self-preserving principle. **It is** probable that **the** truly helpful men of the next hundred years will occupy themselves very much with the physical welfare of the race, without which no other welfare is possible.

INEBRIATE ASYLUMS, AND A VISIT TO ONE.

THERE are two kinds of drunkards, — the Regular and the Occasional. Of each of these two classes there are several varieties, and, indeed, there are no two cases precisely alike ; but every drunkard in the world is either a person who has lost the power to refrain from drinking a certain large quantity of alcoholic liquor every day, or he is one who has lost the power to refrain from drinking an uncertain enormous quantity now and then.

Few get drunk habitually who can refrain. If they could refrain, they would ; for to no creatures is drunkenness so loathsome and temperance so engaging as to seven tenths of the drunkards. There are a few very coarse men, of heavy, stolid, animal organization, who almost seem formed by nature to absorb alcohol, and in whom there is not enough of manhood to be ashamed of its degradation. These Dr. Albert Day, the superintendent of the New York State Inebriate Asylum, sometimes calls Natural Drunkards. They like strong drink for its own sake ; they have a kind of sulky enjoyment of its muddling effect upon such brains as they happen to have; and when once the habit is fixed, nothing can deliver them except stone walls and iron bars. There are also a few drunkards of very light calibre, trifling persons, incapable of serious reflection or of a serious purpose, their very terrors being trivial and transitory, who do not care for the ruin in which they are involved. Generally speaking, however, drunkards hate the servitude into which they have had the misfortune to fall; they long to escape from it, have often tried to escape, and if they have given up, it is only after having so many times slidden back into the abyss, that they feel it would be of no use to climb again. As Mrs. H. B. Stowe remarks, with that excellent charity of hers, which is but another name for refined justice, "Many a drunkard has expended more virtue in vain endeavors to break his chain than suffices to carry an ordinary Christian to heaven."

The daily life of one of the steady drunkards is like this: upon getting up in the morning, after a heavy, restless, drunkard's sleep, he is miserable beyond expression, and almost helpless. In very bad cases, he will see double, and his hands will tremble so that he cannot lift to his lips the glass for which he has a desire amounting to mania. Two or three stiff glasses of spirituous liquor will restore him so far that he can control his muscles, and get about without betraying his condition. After being up an hour, and drinking every ten or fifteen minutes, he will usually be able to eat a pretty good breakfast, which, with the aid of coffee, tobacco, and a comparatively small quantity of liquor, he will be able to digest. After breakfast, for some hours he will generally be able to transact routine business, and associate with his fellows without exciting their pity or contempt. As dinner-time draws near he feels the necessity of creating an appetite; which he often accomplishes by drinking some of those infernal compounds which are advertised on the eternal rocks and mountain-sides as Bitters, — a mixture of bad drugs with worse spirits. These bitters do lash the torpid powers into a momentary, morbid, fierce activity, which enables the victim to eat even a superabundant dinner. The false excitement subsides, but the dinner remains, and it has to be digested. This calls for an occasional drink for three or four hours, after which the system is exhausted, and the man feels dull and languid. **He is** exhausted, but he is not tranquil; he craves a continuation of the stimulant with a craving which human nature, so abused and perverted, never resists. By this time it is evening, when all the apparatus of temptation is in the fullest activity, and all the loose population of the town is abroad. He now begins his evening debauch, and keeps up a steady drinking until he can drink no more, when he stumbles home to **sleep** off the stupefying fumes, and awake to the horror and decrepitude of a drunkard's morning.

The quantity of spirituous liquor required to keep one of these unhappy men in this degrading slavery varies from a pint a day to two quarts. Many drunkards consume a quart of whiskey every day for years. The regular allowance of one gentleman of the highest position, both social and official, who made his way to the Inebriate Asylum, had been two quarts of brandy a day for about five years. The most remarkable known case is that of a hoary-headed man of education and fortune, residing in the city of New York, who confesses to taking "fifty drinks a day" of whiskey,— ten drinks to a bottle, and five bottles to a gallon. One gallon of liquor, he *says*, goes down his old throat every day of the year. Before he is fit to eat his breakfast in the morning he has to drink twelve glasses of whiskey, or one bottle and one fifth. Nevertheless, even this poor man is able, for some hours of the morning, to transact what people of property and leisure call business, and, during a part of the evening, to converse in such a way as to amuse persons who can look on and see a human being in such bondage without stopping to think what a tragedy it is. This Old Boy never has to be carried home, I believe. He is one of those most hopeless drunkards who never get drunk, never wallow in the gutter, never do anything to scare or startle them into an attempt to reform. He is like a certain German "puddler" who was pointed out to me in a Pittsburg iron-works, who consumes exactly seven dollars' worth of lager-bier every seven days,— twenty glasses a day, at five cents each. He is also like the men employed in the dismal work of the brewery, who are allowed as much beer as they can drink, and who generally do drink as much as they can. Such persons are always fuddled and stupid, but seldom drunk enough to alarm their neighbors or themselves. Perhaps they are the only persons in all the world who are in any degree justified in passing their lives in a state of suspended intelligence; those of them at least whose duty it is to get inside of enormous beer barrels, and there, in darkness and solitude, in an atmosphere reeking and heavy with stale ale, scrape and mop them out before they are refilled. When you see their dirty, pale faces at the "man-hole" of the barrel, down in the rumbling bowels of the earth, in one of those vast caves of beer in Cincinnati, you catch yourself saying, "Drink, poor devils, drink! Soak what brains you have in beer!" What can a man want with brains in a beer-barrel? But then, you think again, even these poor men need their brains when they get home; and *we* need that they should have brains on the first Tuesday in November.

It is that *going home* which makes drunkenness so dire a tragedy. If the drunkard could only shut himself up with a whiskey-barrel, or a pipe of Madeira, and quietly guzzle himself to death, it would be a pity, but it could be borne. **He** never does this; he goes home to make that home perdition to some good souls that love him, or depend upon him, and cannot give him up. There are men at the Asylum near Binghamton, who have admirable wives, beautiful **and** accomplished daughters, venerable parents, whose portraits **are there** in the patient's trunks, and who write **daily** letters to cheer the absent one, whose absence now, for the first time in years, does not terrify them. *They* are the victims of drunkenness, — they who never taste strong drink. For *their* deliverance, this Asylum stands upon its hill justified in existing. The men themselves are interesting, valuable, precious, worth every rational effort that can be made to save them ; but it is those whom they left at home anxious and desolate that have the first claim upon our consideration.

With regard to these steady, regular drunkards, the point to be noted is this: very few of them can stop drinking while they continue to perform their daily labor; they absolutely *depend* upon the alcohol to rouse their torpid energies to activity. Their jaded constitutions will not budge without the spur. Everything within them gapes and hungers for the accustomed stimulant. This is the case, even in a literal sense; for it seems, from Dr. Day's dissections, that the general effect of excessive drinking is to enlarge the globules of which the brain, the blood, the liver, and other organs are composed, so that those globules, as it were, stand open-mouthed, empty, athirst, inflamed, and most eager to be filled. A man whose every organ is thus diseased cannot usually take the first step toward cure without ceasing for a while to make any other demands upon himself. This is the great fact of his condition. If he is a true drunkard, i. e. if he has lost the power to do his work without excessive alcoholic stimulation, then there is no cure possible for him without rest. Here we have the simple explanation of Mrs. Stowe's fine remark **just** quoted. This is why so many thousand wives **spend** their days in torment between hope and despair,— hope kindled by the husband's efforts to regain possession of himself, and despair caused by his repeated, his inevitable relapses. The unfortunate man tries to do two things at once, the easiest of which is as much as he can accomplish; while the hardest is a task which, even with the advantage of perfect rest, few can perform without assistance.

The Occasional Drunkard is a man who is a teetotaler for a week, two weeks, a month, three months, six months, and who, at the end of his period, is tempted to drink one glass of alcoholic liquor. That one glass has upon him two effects; it rouses the slumbering demon of Desire, and it perverts his moral judgment. All at once his honor and good name, **the** happiness and dignity of his family, his success in business, all that he held dearest a moment before, seem small to him, and he thinks he has been a fool of late to concern himself so much about them. Or else he thinks he can drink without being found out, and without its doing **him** the harm it did the last time. Whatever may be the particular delusion that seizes him, the effect **is** the **same**; he drinks, **and** drinks, and drinks, keeping **it up** sometimes for **ten** days, or even for several weeks, until the long **debauch** ends in utter exhaustion **or in delirium tremens.** He is then compelled to **submit** to treatment; **he must** needs go to the Inebriate Asylum of his own bedroom. There, whether he raves or droops, he is the most miserable wretch on earth; for, besides the bodily tortures which he suffers, he has to endure the most desolating pang that a decent human being ever knows,—the loss of his self-respect. He abhors himself and is ashamed; he remembers past relapses and despairs; he cannot look his own children in the face; he wishes he had never been born, or had died in the cursed hour, vividly remembered, when this appetite mastered him first. As his health is restored, his hopes revive; he renews his resolution and he resumes his ordinary routine, subdued, distrustful of himself, and on the watch against temptation. Why he again relapses he can hardly tell, but he always does. Sometimes a snarl in business perplexes him, and he drinks for elucidation. Sometimes melancholy oppresses him, and he drinks to drive dull care away. Sometimes good fortune overtakes him, or an enchanting day in June or October attunes his heart to joy, and he is taken captive by the strong delusion that now is the time to drink and be glad. Often it is lovely woman who offers the wine, and offers it in such a way that he thinks he cannot refuse without incivility or confession. From conversation with the inmates of the Inebriate Asylum, I am confident that Mr. Greeley's assertion with regard to the wine given at the Communion is correct. That sip might be enough to awaken the desire. The mere odor of the wine filling the church might be too much for some men.

There appears to be a physical cause for this extreme susceptibility. Dr. Day has once had the opportunity to examine the brain of a man who, after having been a drunkard, reformed, and lived for some years a teetotaler. He found, to his surprise, that the globules of the brain had not shrunk to their natural size. They did not exhibit the inflammation of the drunkard's brain, but they were still enlarged, and seemed ready on the instant to absorb the fumes of alcohol, and resume their former condition. He thought he saw in this morbid state of the brain the physical part of the reason why a man who has once been a drunkard can never again, as long as he lives, safely take one drop of any alcoholic liquor. He thought he saw why a glass of wine puts the man back instantly to where he was when he drank all the time. He saw the citadel free from the enemy, swept and clean, but undefended, incapable of defence, and its doors opened wide to the enemy's return; so that there was no safety, except in keeping the foe at a distance, away beyond the outermost wall.

There are many varieties of these occasional drunkards, and, as a class, they are perhaps the hardest to cure. Edgar Poe was one of them; half a glass of wine would set him off upon a wild, reckless debauch, that would last for days. All such persons as artists, writers, and actors used to be particularly subject to this malady, before they had any recognized place in the world, or any acknowledged right to exist at all. Men whose labors are intense, but irregular, whose gains are small and uncertain, who would gladly be gentlemen, but are compelled to content themselves with being loafers, are in special danger; and so are men whose toil is extremely monotonous. Printers, especially those who work at night upon newspapers, are, perhaps, of all men the most liable to fall under the dominion of drink. Some of them have persuaded themselves that they rest under a kind of necessity to "go on a tear" now and then, as a relief from such grinding work as theirs. On the contrary, one "tear" creates the temptation to another; for the man goes back to his work weak, depressed, and irritable; the monotony of his labor is aggravated by the incorrectness with which he does it, and the longing to break loose and renew the oblivion of drink strengthens rapidly, until it masters him once more.

Of these periodical drunkards it is as true as it is of their regular brethren, that they cannot conquer the habit without being relieved for a while of their daily labor. This malady is so frequent among us, that hardly an individual will cast his eyes over these pages who cannot call to mind at least one person who has struggled with it for many years, and struggled in vain. They attempt too much. Their periodical "sprees," "benders," or "tears" are a connected series, each a cause and an effect, an heir and a progenitor. After each debauch, the man returns to his routine in just the state of health, in just the state of mind, to be irritated, disgusted, and exhausted by that routine; and, at every moment of weakness, there is always present the temptation to seek the deadly respite of alcohol. The moment arrives when the desire becomes too strong for him, and the victim yields to it by a law as sure, as irresistible, as that which makes the apple seek the earth's centre when it is disengaged from the tree.

It is amazing to see how helpless men can be against such a habit, while they are compelled to continue their daily round of duties. Not ignorant men only, nor bad men, nor weak men, but men of good understanding, of rare gifts, of the loftiest aspirations, of characters the most amiable, engaging, and estimable, and of will sufficient for every purpose but this. They *know* the ruin that awaits them, or in which they are already involved, better than we other sinners know it; they hate their bondage worse than the most uncharitable of their friends can despise it; they look with unutterable envy upon those who still have dominion over themselves; many, very many of them would give all they have for deliverance; and yet self-deliverance is impossible. There are men among them who have been trying for thirty years to abstain, and still they drink. Some of them have succeeded in lengthening the sober interval, and they will live with strictest correctness for six months or more, and then, taking that first fatal glass, will immediately lose their self-control, and drink furiously for days and nights; drink until they are obliged to use drunken artifice to get the liquid into their mouths, — their hands refusing their office. Whether they take a large quantity of liquor every day, or an immense quantity periodically, makes no great **difference, the** disease is essentially the **same;** the difficulties in the way of cure **are the same;** the remedial measures must be the same. A drunkard, in short, **is** a person so diseased by alcohol, that he cannot get through his work without keeping his system saturated with it, or with**out such** weariness and irritation as furnish irresistible temptation **to a debauch. He** is, in other words, a fallen brother, who cannot get upon his feet without help, and **who can** generally get upon his feet with help.

Upon this truth Inebriate Asylums are founded; their object being to afford the help needed. There are now four such institutions in **the** United States: one in Boston, opened in 1857, called the Washingtonian **Home;** one in Media, near Philadelphia, opened in 1867, called the Sanitarium; one at Chicago, opened in 1868; and one at Binghamton, New York, called the New York Inebriate Asylum. The **one** last named was founded in 1858, if the laying of the corner-stone with grand ceremonial can be called founding it; and it has been opened some years for **the** reception of patients; but it had no real existence as **an** asylum for the cure of inebriates until the year 1867, when the present superintendent, **Dr.** Albert Day, assumed control.

The history of the institution previous to that time ought to be related **fully** for the warning of a preoccupied and subscribing **public,** but space cannot be afforded for it here. The substance **of it,** as developed in sundry reports of trials and pamphlets of testimony, is this: Fifteen or twenty years ago, an English adventurer living in the city of New York, calling himself a doctor, and professing to treat unnamable diseases, thought he saw in this notion of an Inebriate Asylum (then much spoken of) a chance for feathering his nest. He entered upon the enterprise without delay, and he displayed a good deal of nervous energy in getting the charter, collecting money, and erecting the building. The people of Binghamton, misled by his representations, gave a farm of two hundred and fifty-two acres for the future inmates to cultivate, which was two hundred acres too much; and to this tract farms still more superfluous have been added, until the Asylum estate contains more than five hundred acres. An edifice was begun on the scale of an imperial palace, which will have cost, by the time it is finished and furnished, a million dollars. The restless man pervaded the State raising money, and creating public opinion in favor of the institution. For several years he was regarded as one of the great originating philanthropists of the age; and this the more because he always gave out that he was laboring in the cause from pure love of the inebriate, and received no compensation.

But the time came when his real object and true character were revealed. In 1864 he carried his disinterestedness so far as to offer to give to the institution, as part of its permanent fund, the entire amount to which he said he was entitled for services rendered and expenses incurred. This amount was two hundred and thirty-two thousand dollars, which would certainly have been a handsome gift. When he was asked for the items of his account, he said he had charged for eighteen years' services in founding the institution, at thirty-five hundred dollars a year, and the rest was travelling-expenses, clerk hire, and salaries paid to agents. The trustees were puzzled to know how a man who, at the beginning of the enterprise, had no visible property, could have expended so much out of his private resources, while exercising an unremunerated employment. Leaving that conundrum unsolved, they were able at length to conjecture the object of the donation. One of the articles of the charter provided that any person giving ten dollars to the institution should be a stockholder, and entitled to a vote at the election of trustees. Every gift of ten dollars was a vote! If, therefore, this astounding claim had been allowed, and the *gift* accepted, the audacious villain would have been constituted owner of four fifths of the governing stock, and the absolute controller of the entire property of the institution! It was a bold game, and the strangest part of the story is, that it came near succeeding. It required the most arduous exertions of a public-spirited board of trustees, headed by Dr. Willard Parker, to oust the man who, even after the discovery of his scheme, played his few last cards so well that he had to be bought off by a considerable sum cash down. An incident of the disastrous reign of this individual was the burning of **one** of the wings of the building, after he had had it **well** insured. The insurance was paid him (**$ 81,000**); and there was **a trial** for arson, — a crime which **is easy** to commit, and hard to prove. **Binghamton** convicted the prisoner, but the jury was obliged to acquit him.*

---

* The man and his confederates must have carried off **an** enormous **booty**. The local trustees say, **in** their Report **for** 1867: —

"Less than two years ago the Asylum received about **$ 81,000** from insurance companies for damage done by fire to **the** north wing. About **$ 20,000** have since been received from the counties; making from these two sources about $ 100,000; and, although the buildings and grounds remain in the same unfinished state as when the fire occurred, except a small amount **of** work done in one or two wards in the south wing, the $ 100,000 have nearly disappeared. . . . . Aside from the payment **of interest** and insurance, this money has been expended by Dr. ——, **and in** just such ways as he thought proper to use it.

"It may well **be** asked why this is so. The **answer is, that** Dr. —— assumes and exercises supreme control, and allows no interference, **at least** on the part of the resident trustees. . . . .

"**His control and** management of everything connected with the institution **has been as** absolute in fact, if not in form, as if he were its **sole** proprietor. He goes to Albany to obtain legislation giving **him** extraordinary police powers, without as much as even informing the trustees of **his** intentions. When the iron grates for the windows of the lower **ward were** obtained, **the** resident trustees knew nothing of the matter, until **they were** informed that the patients **were** looking through barred **windows**. Everything has been **done** in the same way. He is not known to have had any **other** official relation to the institution by regular appointment than that **of corresponding** secretary, and yet he has exercised a power over its **affairs** which has defied all re-

Such things may be done in a community where almost every one is benevolent enough to give money towards an object that promises to mitigate human woe, but where scarcely any one has leisure to watch the expenditure of that sacred treasure!

The institution, after it was open, remained for two years under the blight of this person's control. Everything he did was wrong. Ignorant, obstinate, passionate, fussy, and false, — plausible and obsequious at Albany, a violent despot at the Asylum, — he was, of all the people in the world, the precisely worst man to conduct an experiment so novel and so abounding in difficulties. If he had a theory, it was that an inebriate is something between a criminal and a lunatic, who is to be punished like the one and restrained like the other. His real object seemed to be, after having received payment for a patient six months in advance, to starve and madden him into a sudden departure. The very name chosen by him for the institution proves his hopeless incompetency. "Inebriate Asylum!" That name to-day is, perhaps, the greatest single obstacle to its growth. He began by affixing a stigma to the unfortunate men who had honored themselves

straint. He lives there with his family, without a salary, and without individual resources, and dispenses hospitality or charity to his kindred with as much freedom and unreserve as if he owned overything and had unlimited means at his command. In fact, incredible as it may seem, he claims that he is virtually the owner of the institution. And his claim might have challenged contradiction, had his plans succeeded."

by making so gallant an effort at **self-recovery**. But let the man and his doings pass into oblivion. There never yet was a bad man who **was** not, upon the whole, a very stupid **ass**. All the genuine intelligence in the **world** resides in virtuous minds. When, therefore, I **have** said that this individual was **an** unprincipled adventurer, I have also said that he was signally incapable of conducting an institution like this.

While **we**, in **the** State of New York, were blundering **on in** this way, permitting **a** million dollars of public and private money to be lavished in the attempt to found an asylum, **a few** quiet **people** in Boston, aided by a small annual grant **from the** Legislature, had actually established one, and **kept it** going for nine years, during **which** three thousand inebriates had been received, and two thousand of them cured! The thing was accomplished **in** the simplest way. They hired the best house for the purpose that chanced to **be vacant**, fitted **it up** at the least possible expense, **installed in it as** superintendent an honest man whose **heart was in** the business, and opened **its** doors for the reception **of** patients. By and by, when they had results to show, **they** asked the Legislature for a little help, which was granted, and **has** been renewed from year to year ever since. The sum voted has **never** exceeded five thousand dollars in any year, and there are three men in Boston at this moment reclaimed from drunkenness **by** the Washingtonian Home who pay taxes enough to support it.

In an enterprise **for** the management of which no

precedents exist, everything of course depends upon the chief. When you have got the right man at the head, you have got everything; and until you have got the right man there, you have got nothing. Albert Day, the superintendent for nine years of the Washingtonian Home at Boston, and during the last year and a half the superintendent of the Asylum at Binghamton, has originated nearly all that is known of the art of curing the mania for alcohol. He struck into the right path at once, guided by instinct and sympathy, rather than by science or reflection. He was not a professional person; he was simply a business man of good New England education, who had two special qualifications for his new position, — first, a singular pity for drunkards; and, secondly, a firm belief that, with timely and right assistance, a majority of them could be restored to self-control. This pity and this faith he had possessed for many years, and they had both grown strong by exercise. When he was a child upon his father's farm in Maine, he saw in his own home and all around him the evils resulting from the general use of alcoholic liquors, so that when the orators of teetotalism came along he was ready to receive their message. He is one of the very few persons now living in the world who never partook of an alcoholic beverage, — so early was he convinced of their preposterous inutility. Losing his father at thirteen, he at once took hold of life in the true Yankee way. He tied up his few worldly effects into a bundle, and, slinging it over his shoulder, walked to a farmer's house not many miles away, and addressed to him a plain question, "Do you want to hire a boy?" to which the farmer with equal directness replied, "Yes." From hoeing corn and chopping wood the lad advanced to an apprenticeship, and learned a mechanical trade; and so made his way to early marriage, decent prosperity, and a seat in the Legislature of Massachusetts. From the age of sixteen he was known, wherever he lived, as a stanch teetotaler, and also as one who would befriend a drunkard after others had abandoned him to his fate.

I once heard Dr. Day relate the occurrence which produced in his mind the conviction that drunkards could be rescued from the domination of their morbid appetite. One evening, when he came home from his work, he heard that a certain Jack Watts, the sot of the neighborhood, was starving with his wife and three young children. After tea he went to see him. In treating this first patient, Albert Day hit upon the very method he has ever since pursued, and so I beg the reader will note the manner in which he proceeded. On entering his cottage he was as polite to him, as considerate of his dignity as head of a household, as he could have been to the first man of the village. "Mr. Watts," said he, after the usual salutations, "I hear you are in straitened circumstances." The man, who was then quite sober, replied: "I am; my two youngest children went to bed crying for food, and I had none to give them. I spent my last three cents over there," pointing to a grog-shop opposite, "and the bar-keeper said to me, as he took the money, says he, 'Jack Watts, you're a fool'; and so I am." Here was a chance for a fine moral lecture. Albert Day indulged in nothing of the kind. He said, "Mr. Watts, excuse me for a few minutes"; and he went out, returning soon with a basket containing some flour, pork, and other materials for a supper. "Now, Mrs. Watts, cook something, and wake your children up, and give them something to eat. I'll call again early in the morning. Good night."

Perfect civility, no reproaches, no lecture, practical help of the kind needed and at the time needed. Observe, too, that the man was in the condition of mind in which patients usually are when they make the *confession* implied in entering an asylum. He was at the end of his tether. He was — to use the language of the bar-room — "dead beat."

When Mr. Day called the next morning, the family had had their breakfast, and Jack Watts smiled benedictions on the man whom he had been wont to regard as his enemy, because he was the declared enemy of Jack Watts's enemy. Now the time had come for a little talk. Jack Watts explained his circumstances; he had been out of work for a long time, and he had consumed all his substance in drink. Mr. Day listened with respectful attention, spoke to him of various plans for the future, and said that for that day he could give him a dollar's worth of wood-chopping to do. Then they got upon the liquor question. In the softened, receptive mind of Jack Watts, Albert Day deposited the substance of a rational temperance lecture. He spoke to him kindly, respectfully, hopefully, strongly. Jack Watts's mind was convinced; he said he had done with drink forever. He meant it too; and thus he was brought to the second stage on the road to deliverance. In this particular case, resting from labor was out of the question and unnecessary, for the man had been resting too long already, and must needs go to work. The wood was chopped. The dollar to be paid for the work at the close of the day was a fearful ordeal for poor Jack, living fifteen yards from a bar-room. Mr. Day called round in the evening, paid him the dollar without remark, fell into ordinary conversation with the family, and took leave. John stood the test; not a cent of the money found its way into the till of the bar-keeper. Next morning Mr. Day was there again, and, seeing that the patient was going on well, spoke to him further about the future, and glided again into the main topic, dwelling much upon the absolute necessity of total and eternal abstinence. He got the man a place, visited him, held him up, fortified his mind, and so helped him to complete and lasting recovery. Jack Watts never drank again. He died a year or two ago in Maine at a good age, having brought up his family respectably.

This was an extreme case, for the man had been a drunkard many years; it was a difficult case, for he was poor and ignorant; and it made upon the mind of Albert Day an impression that nothing could efface. He was living in Boston in 1857, exercising his trade, when the Washingtonian Home was opened. He was indeed one of the originators of the movement, and took the post of superintendent because no one else seemed capable of conducting the experiment. Having now to deal with the diseased bodies of men, he joined the medical department of Harvard University, and went through the usual course, making a particular study of the malady he was attempting to cure. After nine years' service he was transferred to the Asylum at Binghamton, where he pursues the system practised with success at Boston.

I visited the Binghamton Asylum in June of the present year. The situation combines many advantages. Of the younger cities that have sprung into importance along the line of leading railroads there is not one of more vigorous growth or more inviting appearance than Binghamton. Indications of spirit and civilization meet the eye at every turn. There are long streets of elegant cottages and villas, surrounded by nicely kept gardens and lawns, and containing churches in the construction of which the established barbarisms have been avoided. There is a general tidiness and attention to appearances that we notice in the beautiful towns and villages of New England; such as picturesque Northampton, romantic Brattleboro', and enchanting Stockbridge, peerless among villages. The Chenango River unites here with the Susquehanna; so that the people who have not a river within sight of their front doors are likely to have one flowing peacefully along at the back of their gardens. It is a town, the existence of which in a State governed as New York is governed shows how powerless a government is to corrupt a virtuous and intelligent people, and speaks of the time when governments will be reduced to their natural and proper insignificance. Such communities require little of the central power; and it is a great pity that that little is indispensable, and that Albany cannot be simply wiped out.

Two miles from Binghamton, on a high hill rising from the bank of the Susquehanna, and commanding an extensive view of the beautiful valleys of both rivers, stands the castellated palace which an adventurer had the impudence to build with money intrusted to him for a better purpose. The Erie Railroad coils itself about the base of this eminence, from the summit of which the white puffs of the locomotive can be descried in one direction nine miles, and in the other fifteen miles. On reaching this summit about nine o'clock on a fine morning in June, I found myself in front of a building of light-colored stone, presenting a front of three hundred and sixty-five feet, in a style of architecture that unites well the useful and the pleasing. Those numerous towers which relieve the monotony of so extensive a front serve an excellent purpose in providing small apartments for various purposes, which, but for them, could not be contrived without wasting space. At present the first view of the building is not inviting, for the burnt wing remains roofless and void, — the insurance money not having been applied to refitting it, — and the main edifice is still unfinished.

Not a tree has yet been planted, and the grounds about the building are little more pleasing to the eye than fifty acres of desert. On a level space in front of the edifice a number of young men were playing a game of base-ball, and playing it badly. Their intentions were excellent, but their skill was small. Sitting on the steps and upon the blocks of stone scattered about were fifty or sixty well-dressed, well-looking gentlemen of various ages, watching the game. In general appearance and bearing these persons were so decidedly superior to the average of mortals, that few visitors fail to remark the fact. Living up there in that keen, pure air, and living in a rational manner, amusing themselves with games of ball, rowing, sailing, gardening, bowling, billiards, and gymnastic exercises, they are as brown and robust as David Copperfield was when he came home from the Continent and visited his friend Traddles. Take any hundred men from the educated classes, and give them a few months of such a life as this, and the improvement in their appearance will be striking. Among these on-lookers of the game were a few men with gray hairs, but the majority were under thirty, perhaps thirty-two or thirty-five was about the average age.

When I looked upon this most unexpected scene, it did not for a moment occur to me that these serene and healthy-looking men could be the inmates of the Asylum. The insensate name of the institution prepares the visitor to see the patients lying about in various stages of intoxication. The question has sometimes been asked of the superintendent by visitors looking about them and peering into remote corners, " But, Doctor, where do you *keep* your drunkards?" The astonishment of such inquirers is great indeed when they are informed that the polite and well-dressed gentlemen standing about, and in whose hearing the question was uttered, are the inmates of the institution; every individual of whom was till very recently, not merely a drunkard, but a drunkard of the most advanced character, for whose deliverance from that miserable bondage almost every one had ceased to hope. A large majority of the present inmates are persons of education and respectable position, who pay for their residence here at rates varying from ten to twenty dollars a week, and who are co-operating ardently with the superintendent for their recovery. More than half of them were officers of the army or navy during the late war, and lost control of themselves then. One in ten must be by law a free patient; and whenever an inebriate really desires to break his chain, he is met half-way by the trustees, and his board is fixed at a rate that accords with his circumstances. A few patients have been taken as low as five dollars a week. When once the building has been completed, the grounds laid out, and the farms disposed of, the trustees hope never to turn from the door of the institution any proper applicant who desires to avail himself of its assistance. The present number of patients is something less than one hundred, which is about fifty less than can be accommodated. When the burnt wing is restored, there will be room for four hundred.

Upon entering the building, we find ourselves in a spacious, handsome, well-arranged, and well-furnished hotel. The musical click of billiard-balls, and the distant thunder of the bowling-alley, salute the ear; one of the inmates may be performing brilliantly on the piano, or trying over a new piece for next Sunday on the cabinet organ in the temporary chapel. The billiard-room, we soon discover, contains three tables. There is a reading-room always open, in which the principal periodicals of both continents, and plenty of newspapers, are accessible to all the patients. A small library, which ought to be a larger one, is open at a certain hour every day. A conservatory is near completion, and there is a garden of ten acres near by in which a number of the inmates may usually be seen at work. A croquet-ground is not wanting, and the apparatus of cricket is visible in one of the halls. The chapel is still far from being finished, but enough is done to show that it will be elegant and inviting soon after the next instalment of excise-money comes in. The dining-room is lofty and large, as indeed are all the public rooms. The private rooms are equal, both in size and furniture, to those of good city hotels. The arrangements for warming, lighting, washing, bathing, cooking, are such as we should expect to find in so stately an edifice. We have not yet reached the point when housework will do itself; but in great establishments like this, where one man, working ten minutes an hour, warms two or three hundred rooms, menial labor is hopefully reduced. In walking about the wide halls and airy public apartments, the visitor sees nothing to destroy the impression that the building is a very liberally arranged summer hotel. To complete the illusion, he will perhaps see toddling about a lovely child with its beautiful mother, and in the large parlor some ladies visiting inmates or officers of the institution. The table also is good and well served. A stranger, not knowing the nature of the institution, might, however, be puzzled to decide whether it is a hotel or a college. No one, it is true, ever saw a college so handsomely arranged and provided ; but the tone of the thing is college-like, especially when you get about among the rooms of the inmates, and see them cramming for next Monday's debate, or writing a lecture for the Asylum course.

This institution is in fact, as in appearance, a rationally conducted hotel or Temporary Home and resting-place for men diseased by the excessive use of alcoholic drinks. It is a place where they can pause and reflect, and gather strength and knowledge for the final victorious struggle with themselves. Temptation is not so remote that their resolution is not in continual exercise, nor so near that it is tasked beyond its strength. There lies Binghamton in its valley below them in plain sight, among its rivers and its trees, with its thousand pretty homes and its dozen nasty bar-rooms. They can go down 'there and drink, if they can get any one to risk the fifty dollars' fine imposed by the law of the State upon any one who sells liquor to an inmate of the Asylum. Generally there is some poor mercenary wretch who will do it. Until it has been proved that the sight of Binghamton is too much for a patient, the only restraint upon his liberty is, that he must not enter the town without the consent of the superintendent. This consent is not regarded in the light of a permission, but in that of a physician's opinion. The patient is supposed to mean: "Dr. Day, would you, as my medical adviser, recommend me to go to Binghamton this morning to be measured for a pair of shoes? Do you think it would be salutary? Am I far enough advanced in convalescence to trust myself to breathe the air of the valley for an hour?" The doctor gives his opinion on the point, and it is etiquette to accept that opinion without remark. Not one patient has yet visited the town, with the consent of the superintendent, who has proved unequal to the temptation. If an inmate steals away and yields to his craving, he is placed in confinement for a day or two, or longer if necessary. It occasionally happens that a patient, conscious of the coming on of a paroxysm of desire, asks to have the key of his room turned upon him till it is over. It is desired that this turning of the key, and those few barred rooms in one of the wards, shall be regarded as mere remedial appliances, as much so as the bottles of medicine in the medicine-chest. It is, however, understood that no one is to be released from confinement who does not manifest a renewed purpose to refrain.

Such a purpose is sometimes indicated by a note addressed to the superintendent like the following, which I happened to see placed in his hands : —

"DR. DAY : —

"DEAR SIR : I cannot let the circumstance which happened yesterday pass by without assuring you that I am truly sorry for the disgrace I have brought on the institution, as well as myself. I certainly appreciate your efforts to guide us all in the right direction, and more especially the interest that you have taken in my own welfare. Let me assure you now, that hereafter, as long as I remain with you, I shall use every endeavor to conduct myself as I should, and cause you no further trouble."

Lapses of this kind are not frequent, and they are regarded by the superintendent as part of the means of restoration which the institution affords; since they aid him in destroying a fatal self-confidence, and in inculcating the idea that a patient who lapses must never think of giving up the struggle, but renew it the instant he can gain the least foothold of self-control.

The system of treatment pursued here is founded on the expectation that the patient and the institution will co-operate. If a man does not desire to be reclaimed, and such a desire cannot be awakened within him, the institution can do no more than keep him sober while he remains an inmate of it. There will, perhaps, one day be in every State an asylum for incurable drunkards, wherein they will be permanently detained, and compelled to live temperately, and earn their subsistence by suitable labor. But this is **not such** an institution. Here all is voluntary. The co-operation of the patient is assumed; and when no desire to be restored **can** be roused, the experiment is not continued longer than a few months.

The **two grand** objects aimed **at by** the superintendent are, to raise the tone **of** the bodily health, **and to** fortify the weakened will. The means employed vary somewhat **in** each case. The superintendent designs **to** make a particular study of each individual; he endeavors to win his confidence, to adapt the treatment to his peculiar disposition, and **to give** him just the aid he needs. As the number of patients increases, this will become more difficult, if it does not become impossible. The more general features of the system are all that can be communicated to others, and these I will endeavor briefly to indicate.

It is interesting to observe the applicants for admission, when they enter the office of the Asylum, accompanied generally by a relative or friend. Some **reach** the building far gone in intoxication, having indulged in one last farewell debauch; or having drunk a bottle of whiskey for the purpose of screwing their courage to the sticking-point of entering the Asylum. A clergyman whom this institution restored told me that he reached Binghamton in the evening, and went to bed drunk; and before going to the Asylum the next morning he had to fortify his system and his resolve by twelve glasses of brandy. Sometimes the accompanying friend, out of an absurd kind of pity for a poor fellow about to be deprived of his solace, will rather encourage him to drink; and often the relatives of an inebriate can only get him into the institution by keeping him intoxicated until he is safe under its roof. Frequently men arrive emaciated and worn out from weeks or months of hard drinking; and occasionally a man will be brought in suffering from delirium tremens, who will require restraint and watching for several days. Some enter the office in terror, expecting to be immediately led away by a turnkey and locked up. All come with bodies diseased and minds demoralized; for the presence of alcohol in the system lowers the tone of the whole man, body and soul, strengthening every evil tendency, and weakening every good one. And this is the reason why men who are brought here against their will are not to be despaired of. Alcohol may only have suspended the activity of their better nature, which a few weeks of total abstinence may rouse to new life. As the health improves, ambition often revives, the native delicacy of the soul reappears, and the man becomes polite, docile, interested, agreeable, who on entering seemed coarse, stupid, obstinate, and malign.

The new-comer subscribes to the rules, pays his board three months in advance, and surrenders all the rest of his money. The paying in advance is a good thing; it is like paying your passage on going on board ship; the voyager has no care, and nothing to think of, but the proposed object. It is also one more inducement to remain until other motives gain strength.

Many hard drinkers live under the conviction that if they should cease drinking alcoholic liquors suddenly, they would die in a few days. This is a complete error. No "tapering off" is allowed here. Dr. Day discovered years ago that a man who has been drinking a quart of whiskey a day for a long time suffers more if his allowance is reduced to a pint than if he is put at once upon the system of total abstinence. He not only suffers less, but for a shorter time. The clergyman before referred to informed me that, for two years and a half before entering the Asylum, he drank a quart of brandy daily, and he felt confident that he would die if he should suddenly cease. He reached Binghamton drunk; he went to bed that evening drunk; he drank twelve glasses of brandy the next morning before eleven o'clock; he went up to the Asylum saturated with brandy, expecting to make the preliminary arrangements for his admission, then return to the hotel, and finish the day drinking. But precisely at that point Albert Day laid his hand upon him, and marked him for his own. Dr. Day quietly objected to his return to the town, sent for his trunk, caused the tavern bill to be paid, and cut off his brandy at once and totally. For forty-eight hours the patient craved the accustomed stimulant intensely, and he was only enabled to sleep by the assistance of bromide of potassium. On the third day the craving ceased, and he assured me that he never felt it again.

Other morbid experiences he had, but not that; and now, after two years of abstinence, he enjoys good health, has no desire for drink, and is capable of extraordinary exertions. Other patients, however, informed me that they suffered a morbid craving for two or three weeks. But all agreed that the sudden discontinuance of the stimulant gave them less inconvenience than they had anticipated, and was in no degree dangerous. It is, indeed, most surprising to see how soon the system begins to rally when once it is relieved of the inimical influence. Complete recovery, of course, is a slow and long effort of nature; but the improvement in the health, feelings, and appearance of patients, after only a month's residence upon that breezy hill, is very remarkable.

There is an impression in the country that the inmates of such asylums as this undergo some mysterious process, and take unknown medicines, which have power to destroy the desire for strong drink. Among the quack medicines of the day is a bottled humbug, pretending to have such power. It is also supposed by some that the plan which Captain Marryat mentions is efficacious, — that of confining a drunken sailor for several days to a diet of beef and brandy. Accounts have gone the rounds of the papers, of another system that consists in saturating with brandy every article of food of which the inebriate partakes. Patients occasionally arrive at the Asylum who expect to be treated in some such way; and when a day or two passes without anything extraordinary or disagreeable happening, they inquire, with visible apprehension, "When the treatment is going to begin." In this sense of the word, there is no treatment here. In all nature there is no substance that destroys or lessens a drunkard's desire for intoxicating liquors; and there is no such thing as permanently disgusting him with brandy by giving him more brandy than he wants. A drunkard's drinking is not a thing of mere appetite; his whole system craves stimulation; and he would drink himself into perdition while loathing the taste of the liquor. This Asylum simply gives its inmates rest, regimen, amusement, society, information. It tries to restore the health and renew the will, and both by rational means.

Merely entering an establishment like this is a long step toward deliverance. It is a confession! It is a confession to the patient's family and friends, to the inmates of the Asylum, and, above all, to himself, that he has lost his self-control, and cannot get it back without assistance. He comes here for that assistance. Every one knows he comes for that. They are all in the same boat. The pot cannot call the kettle black. False pride, and all the thin disguises of self-love, are laid aside. The mere fact of a man's being an inmate of an inebriate asylum is a declaration to all about him that he has been a drunkard, and even a very bad drunkard; for the people here know, from their own bitter experience, that a person cannot bring himself to make such a confession until, by many a lapse, he has been brought to despair of self-recovery. Many of these men were thinking of the asylum for years before they could summon courage to own that they had lost the power to resist a physical craving. But when once they have made the agonizing avowal by entering the asylum, it costs them no great effort to reveal the details of their case to hearers who cannot reproach them; and, besides relating their own experience without reserve, they are relieved, encouraged, and instructed by hearing the similar experience of others. All have the same object, the same peril, the same dread, the same hope, and each aids the rest as students aid one another in the same college.

In a community like this, Public Opinion is the controlling force. That subtle, resistless power is always aiding or frustrating the object for which the community exists. Public Opinion sides with a competent superintendent, and serves him as an assiduous, omnipresent police. Under the coercive system once attempted here, the public opinion of the Asylum applauded a man who smuggled a bottle of whiskey into the building, and invited his friends into his room to drink it. An inmate who should now attempt such a crime would be shunned by the best two thirds of the whole institution. One of their number, suddenly overcome by temptation, who should return to the Asylum drunk, they would all receive as cordially as before; but they would regard with horror or contempt a man who should bring temptation into the building, and place it within reach of those who had fled hither to avoid it.

The French have a verb,—*se dépayser*,—to uncountry one's self, to get out of the groove, to drop undesirable companions and forsake haunts that are too alluring, by going away for a while, and, in returning, not resuming the old friends and habits. How necessary this is to some of the slaves of alcohol every one knows. To many of them restoration is impossible without it, and not difficult with it. To all such, what a refuge is a well-conducted asylum like this! Merely being here, out of the coil of old habits, haunts, pleasures, comrades, temptations, which had proved too much for them a thousand times,—merely being away for a time, so that they can calmly survey the scenes they have left and the life they have led,—is itself half the victory.

Every Wednesday evening, after prayers, a kind of temperance meeting is held in the chapel. It is the intention of the superintendent, that every inmate of the Asylum shall become acquainted with the nature of alcohol, and with the precise effects of alcoholic drinks upon the human system. He means that they shall comprehend the absurdity of drinking as clearly as they know its ruinous consequences. He accordingly opens this meeting with a short lecture upon some one branch of the subject, and then invites the patients to illustrate the point from their own experience. At the meeting which I happened to attend the subject of Dr. Day's remarks was suggested (as it often is) by an occurrence which had just taken place at the institution, and had been the leading topic of conversation all that day. At the last meeting, a young man from a distant State, who had been in the Asylum for some months and was about to return home, delivered an eloquent farewell address to his companions, urging them to adhere to their resolution, and protesting his unalterable resolve never, never, never again to yield to their alluring and treacherous foe. He spoke with unusual animation and in a very loud voice. He took his departure in the morning, by the Erie Road, and twelve hours after he was brought back to the Asylum drunk. Upon his recovery he related to the superintendent and to his friends the story of his lamentable fall. When the train had gone three hours on its way, there was a detention of three hours at a station that offered little entertainment to impatient travellers. The returning prodigal paced the platform; found it dull work; heard at a distance the sound of billiard-balls; went and played two games, losing both; returned to the platform and resumed his walk; and there fell into the train of thought that led to the catastrophe. His reflections were like these: "How perfect is my cure! I have not once *thought* of taking a drink. Not even when I saw men drinking at the bar did it cross my mind to follow their example. I have not the least desire for whiskey, and I have no doubt I could take that 'one glass' which Dr. Day keeps talking about, without a wish for a second. In fact, no man is perfectly cured till he can do that. I have a great mind to put it to the test. It almost seems as if this opportunity of trying myself had been created on purpose. Here goes, then, for the last glass of whiskey I shall take as long as I live, and I take it purely as a scientific experiment." One hour after, his friend, who was accompanying him home, found him lying in a corner of a bar-room, dead drunk. He had him picked up, and placed in the next train bound for Binghamton.

This was the text of Dr. Day's discourse, and he employed it in enforcing anew his three cardinal points: 1. No hope for an inebriate until he thoroughly distrusts the strength of his own resolution; 2. No hope for an inebriate except in total abstinence as long as he lives, both in sickness and in health; 3. Little hope for an inebriate unless he avoids, on system and on principle, the occasions of temptation, the places where liquor is sold, and the persons who will urge it upon him. Physicians, he said, were the inebriate's worst enemies; and he advised his hearers to avoid the tinctures prepared with alcohol, which had often awakened the long-dormant appetite. During my stay at Binghamton, a clergyman resident in the town, and recently an inmate of the Asylum, had a slight indisposition resulting from riding home from a meeting ten miles in the rain. One of the physicians of the place, who knew his history, knew that he had been an inebriate of the most pronounced type (quart of liquor a day), prescribed a powerful dose of brandy and laudanum. "I dare not take it, doctor," he said, and put the damnable temptation behind him. "If I *had* taken it," said he to me, "I should have been drunk to-day." The case, too, required nothing but rest, rice, and an easy book. No medicine was necessary. Dr. Day has had under his care a man who, after being a confirmed drunkard, had been a teetotaler for eighteen years, and had then been advised to take wine for the purpose of hastening a slow convalescence. His appetite resumed its old ascendency, and, after drinking furiously for a year, he was brought to the Asylum in delirium tremens. Dr. Day expressed a strong hope and belief that the returned inmate mentioned above had *now* actually taken his last glass of whiskey; for he had discovered his weakness, and was in a much more hopeful condition than he had been before his lapse. The Doctor scouted the idea that a man who has the misfortune to break his resolution should give up the struggle. Some men, he said, *must* fall, at least once, before the last rag of self-confidence is torn from them; and he had had patients who, after coming back to him in Boston four times, had conquered, and had lived soberly for years, and were still living soberly.

When the superintendent had finished his remarks, he called upon his hearers to speak. Several of them did so. One young gentleman, an officer of the army during the war, made his farewell speech. He thanked his companions for the forbearance they had shown him during the first weeks of his residence among them, when he was peevish, discontented, rebellious, and had no hope of ever being able to conquer his propensity, so often had he tried and failed. He would have left the Asylum in those days, if he had had the money to pay his fare on the cars. He felt the importance of what Dr. Day had advanced respecting the occasions of temptation, and especially what he had said about physicians' prescriptions, which he knew had led men to drink. "If," he added, "I cannot live without alcohol, I would rather die. For my part, I expect to have a struggle all my life; I don't think the time will ever come when it will be safe for me to dally with temptation, and I feel the necessity of following Dr. Day's advice on this point." He spoke in a simple, earnest, and manly manner. He was followed by another inmate, a robust, capable-looking man of thirty-five, who also spoke with directness and simplicity. He hoped that fear would help him to abstain. If he could only keep sober, he had the best possible prospects; but if he again gave way he saw nothing before him but infamy and destruction. He spoke modestly and anxiously, evidently feeling that it was more than a matter of life and death to him. When he had concluded, a young gentleman rose, and delivered a fluent, flowery address upon temperance; just such a discourse as might precede a lapse into drinking.

On Monday evening of every week, the Literary Society of the institution holds its meeting, when essays are read and lectures delivered. The course of lectures delivered last winter are highly spoken of by those who heard them, and they were all written by inmates of the Asylum. Among the subjects treated were: Columbus, a Study of Character; Goldsmith; The Telegraph, by an Operator; Resources of Missouri; Early English Novelists; The Age, and the Men for the Age; Geology; The Passions, with Poetical Illustrations; The Inebriate Asylum, under the Régime of Coercion. It occasionally happens, that distinguished visitors contribute something to the pleasure of the evening. Mrs. Stowe, the newspapers inform us, was kind enough some time since to give them a reading from Uncle Tom's Cabin; and the copy of the book from which she read was a cheap double-columned pamphlet brought from the South by a freedman, now the porter of the Asylum. He bought it and read it while he was still a slave, little thinking when he scrawled his name across the dingy title-page that he should ever have the honor of lending it to the authoress.

Nearly twelve years have now elapsed since Dr. Day began to accumulate experience in the treatment of inebriates, during which time he has had nearly four thousand patients under his care. What proportion of these were permanently cured it is impossible to say, because nothing is heard of many patients after they leave; but it is reasonably conjectured that two thirds of the whole number were restored. It is a custom with many of them to write an annual letter to Dr. Day on the anniversary of their entering the Home under his management, and the reading of such letters is a highly interesting and beneficial feature of the Wednesday evening temperance meetings.

The alcoholic mania is no respecter of persons. Dr. Day has had under treatment twenty-one clergymen, one of whom was a Catholic priest (who had delirium tremens), and one a Jewish Rabbi. He has had one old man past seventy, and one boy of sixteen. He has had a Philadelphia "killer" and a judge of a supreme court. He has had steady two-quarts-a-day men, and men who were subject only to semiannual debauches. He has had men whose "tears" lasted but forty-eight hours, and one man who came in of his own accord after what he styled "a general spree" of three months' continuance. He has had drunkards of two years' standing, and those who have been slaves of strong drink for thirty years.

Some of his successes have been striking and memorable. There was Dr. X—— of Tennessee, at thirty-five a physician of large practice, professor in a medical college, happy in an excellent wife and seven children. Falling into drink, he lost at length his practice, his professorship, his property, his home; his family abandoned him to his fate, and went to his wife's father's in another State; and he became at last a helpless gutter sot. His brother, who heard by chance of the Home in Boston, picked him up one day from the street, where he lay insensible, and got him upon the train for the East. Before he roused from his drunken stupor, he was half-way across Virginia. "Where am I?" he asked. "In Virginia, on your way to Boston." "All right," said he, in a drunkard's drunkenest manner,—"all right! give me some whiskey." He was carried into the Home in the arms of men, and lay for some weeks miserably sick. His health improved, and the *man* revived. He clutched at this unexpected chance of escape, and co-operated with all his heart with the system. Dr. Day wrote a hopeful letter to his wife. "Speak not to me of a husband," she replied; "I have no husband; I buried **my** husband long ago." After four months' stay in the institution, the patient returned home, and resumed his practice. A year after, his family rejoined him. He recovered all his former standing, which to this day, after nine years of sobriety, he retains. His ninth annual letter to his deliverer I have read. " By the way," he says in a postscript, "did you receive my letters each year of **the** war?" Yes, they reached Dr. Day months after they were written; but they always reached him. The secret of this cure, as the patient has often asserted, was total abstinence. He had attempted to reduce his daily quantity a hundred times; but never, until he entered the Home, was he aware of the physical *impossibility* of a drunkard's becoming a moderate drinker. From the moment when he had a clear, intellectual comprehension of that truth, the spell was broken: abstinence was easy; he was himself again.

Then there was Y——, a Philadelphia street savage,—one of those firemen who used to sleep in the engine-house, and lie **in wait** for rival companies, and make night and day hideous with slaughter. Fearful beings were those Philadelphia firemen of twenty years ago! Some of them made a nearer approach to total depravity than any creatures I have ever seen that wore the form of man, — revelling in blood, exulting in murder, and glorying in hellish blows with iron implements, given and received. It was difficult to say whether it gave them keener delight to wound or to be wounded. In all communities where external observances and decorums become tyrannical, and where the innocent pleasures of youth are placed under a ban, there is sure to be a class which revolts against the invisible despot, and goes to a horrid extreme of violence and vice. This Y—— was one of the revolters. Once in many weeks he would return to his decent home, ragged and penniless, to be reclothed. It is only alcohol that supports men in a life of *wanton* violence like this; and he, accordingly, was a deep and reckless drinker. His sister prevailed upon him, after many months of persuasion, to go to the Home in Boston, and he presented himself there one morning, black all over with coal-dust. He explained his appearance by saying that he had come from Philadelphia in a coal-vessel. Dr. Day, who had been notified of his coming, received him with that emphatic politeness which produces such magical effects upon men who have long been accustomed to see an enemy in every one who behaves decently and uses the English language in its simplicity. He was exceedingly astonished to be treated with consideration, and to discover that he was not to be sub-

www.ingramcontent.com/pod-product-compliance
Lightning Source LLC
Chambersburg PA
CBHW020056170426
43199CB00009B/306